US, Tak Yokoo sketches a quick and legible roadmap for better collaboration and practical guide to bridging cultural gaps. A smart and compelling read, filled with genuinely funny anecdotes as well as thought-provoking insights into deeper reasons for our differences in how we approach the engineer's bench. Clearly a book written with an appreciation and love for both cultures, and highly recommended for engineers and any other team member of these emerging hybrid-global enterprises, and indeed any student of the corporate culture of Japan or the US.

Brian Swords | Executive Advisor to Japan-affiliated Firms, Former Senior Advisor to Economic Affairs, Consulate General of Japan, Los Angeles

In the age of AI, this book turns frustration into forward nomentum, showing how hybrid teams can surpass any ingle culture through deeply human understanding and isciplined dialogue. Woven throughout is Mr. Yokoo's entle sensitivity, quiet passion, and love of music—an rnest invitation to believe that harmony, once felt, can vel beyond borders.

Ken Satoh | Deputy Director, New Energy and Industrial Technology Development Organization

thoughtful and humane exploration of engineering ond technical skill. Yokoo shows that collaboration is ofessional discipline that deserves as much attention novation.

Dr. Jimmy Chen | Managing Director, Stanford gy, Precourt Institute for Energy, Stanford Doerr School of Sustainability

Praise

Blending engineering rigor with cultural intelligen
this book equips professionals to navigate cross-cult
collaboration with greater awareness and effectivenes
is both strategic and practical.

Terry Tamminen | President and CEO, Alt
Secretary California Environmental Prot
Agency for Governor Arnold Schwarze

An easy-to-follow well written guide on how to n
relationships with Japanese engineers - I wish
before I started working with some of the brigh
in my industry. Highly recommended to anyone
with Japanese firms or who wishes to better und
of the richest cultures on our planet.

Alex Spataru | Found
The Adept Group, Inc., Gradua
UCLA School o

At this moment in history, the US and Ja
in each other as never before. Geopoliti
chains, and the complementary nature of
are fostering joint-ventures, acquisitic
FDI investments at record levels. With
of Japan's FDI employment in the U
and high-value-added products, the e
at the center.

As one of Toyota's most brillian
recent retirement, heading cuttir

Yokoo demonstrates how understanding cultural nuance is essential for unlocking the full innovative potential of Japanese engineering teams. His real-world cases offer leaders practical tools to drive better outcomes across global projects

Dr. James Wallace | AMD UK
Gibb Medical and Rescue

As someone who has spent years building bridges across the world's most formidable cultural and religious divides, I know fi rsthand that genuine understanding, not surface-level tolerance, but deep, earned understanding, is the hardest and most important work there is. Takehito Yokoo has done that work. *The Art of Working with Japanese Engineers* is not merely a professional guide; it is a masterclass in seeing the world through another's eyes. The values Yokoo celebrates, humility, fairness, honor, and collective responsibility, are not foreign to those of us shaped by faith. They are the universal vocabulary of human dignity. This book will make you a better engineer, a better colleague, and, I would argue, a better human being.

Carl Grant III | Author,
How to Live the Abundant Life

Rooted in decades at Toyota and in international clean energy initiatives, this book off ers rare credibility. Yokoo translates complex cultural dynamics into clear and respectful strategies.

Shawn Johal | Business Growth Coach, Elevation Leaders, Bestselling Author of The Happy Leader

Yokoo's leadership in fuel cell innovation lends credibility to every lesson. He understands how advanced technology and human dynamics intersect in high-stakes engineering environments.

Aaron Poynton | Co-Founder and Chairman
of the American Society for AI

Grounded in deep technical expertise and cross-cultural leadership, this book offers practical guidance for improving collaboration between US and Japanese engineering teams. It reflects experience at the highest levels of innovation.

Tamara Nall | CEO & Founder, The Leading Niche

An essential resource for multinational engineering teams. It equips professionals to work smarter together, not harder.

Kumar R. Parakala | CEO, Board Director, USA
National best-selling author, *Lead to Disrupt*

Insightful and actionable. Yokoo explains how process, risk, and communication are viewed differently, and how teams can align those perspectives effectively.

Cory Procter | Author, *Built Not Broke*

By tracing how cultures evolve over long periods, this book shows how deeply rooted patterns shape teamwork, risk decisions, and long-term outcomes, fostering more meaningful cross-cultural understanding.

Alex Melen | Co-Founder, SmartSites

THE ART
OF WORKING WITH JAPANESE ENGINEERS

TAKEHITO YOKOO

Leaders Press

Published in the United States by Leaders Press.

ISBN **978-1-63735-409-4** (pbk)
ISBN **978-1-63735-410-0** (hcv)
ISBN **978-1-63735-408-7** (ebook)

Library of Congress Control Number: **2026901152**

Table of Contents

Acknowledgments

After beginning my career, I was fortunate to work at **Toyota Motor Corporation's Higashi-Fuji Technical Center**, where I was nurtured as an engineer and taught the ways of Japanese society. I extend my sincere gratitude to all the colleagues and mentors who worked alongside me there.

Equally, I am deeply thankful to my colleagues at **Toyota North American Hydrogen Headquarters** in Los Angeles, who have supported me from the time I arrived thirty-five years ago to this day. Even when my English was far from fluent, they welcomed me warmly, respected me, and stood by me as I adapted to a new culture and built both my professional and personal life in the United States.

Regarding the publication of this book, I wish to express my heartfelt appreciation to **Mr. Kevin Beaty**, President and Principal of **YUNEV LLC**. His extensive experience working with Japanese corporations, as well as with teams from China, Korea, and other parts of Asia, provided me with invaluable insights and advice that greatly enriched this work.

I am also deeply indebted to **Mr. Brian Swords**, who served at the **Consulate-General of Japan** in Los Angeles for over thirty-three years, concluding his service in 2023, and who was awarded **the Order of the Sacred Treasure, Gold and Silver Rays** by the Government of Japan in the autumn of 2024. Through his wide network across California and beyond, he introduced me to numerous US government and diplomatic circles and taught me much about American customs and traditions. His thoughtful guidance helped me refine the central message of this book, especially the importance and meaning of the partnership between Japan and the US in today's world.

My decision to leave Japan, build a life in the US, and immerse myself in a culture so different from my own would never have been possible without the guidance of my late father, **Tsuneo Yokoo**, and the unwavering support of my late mother, **Fujiko Yokoo**. When I was still a young boy, my father encouraged me to look beyond Japan and go to America. To live there, to learn from the West, and to grow as a person. His words shaped the path I would take. I also owe deep gratitude to my late elementary school principal, **Mr. Mizuhiko Sato**, who told me during my junior high school years, "There is more than one path up Mount Fuji. You don't have to follow the road everyone else takes. Find your own." His words gave me the courage to walk my own path, and I remain profoundly thankful to him.

I am deeply grateful to my brother and sister-in-law, **Yoshihito Yokoo** and **Keiko Yokoo**, who fully supported my decision to move to the US and assumed responsibility for caring for our parents in Japan. Thanks to their support, I have been able to live abroad for the past thirty-five years without burden, making this book possible.

Finally, and most importantly, I would like to express my deepest gratitude to my wife, **Jullian Yokoo, a realtor, real estate consultant, investor, President of Jozen Power, and Vice President of The Global Engineers Initiative**. Through Jozen Power, the company we founded together, we are contributing to American innovation and working toward a cleaner, more sustainable future. Her unwavering support, thoughtful review of my manuscript, and profound understanding of the Japanese culture in which she was born and raised have guided me every step of the way. Words cannot fully express how grateful I am.

Prologue

I was born in 1957 and grew up in Tokyo from early childhood through my university years. When I was in elementary school, our house still had a well in the yard. We would draw water from it and carry it to the bath, heating the tub with firewood and coal. Very few families owned automobiles at the time.

I remember when the first household electronic calculator was released while I was still in elementary school. It was larger than today's laptop computers, capable of performing only four basic operations with up to twenty digits. My father told me it cost 300,000 yen, an enormous sum sixty years ago. Even when I started working after graduating from university, there were neither mobile phones nor personal computers. The first Apple computer I ever owned had a memory capacity of eight megabytes. Today's MacBooks have sixteen gigabytes, which is a 2,000-fold increase in just thirty-five years.

Reflecting on how much our living environment has changed since those days, it becomes clear that the driving force behind these unimaginable technological innovations, and the acceleration of that progress, has been us, the engineers. It goes without saying that the creation of new technologies by engineers has been vital and invaluable to human advancement.

Being able to spend my life as an engineer—a profession dedicated to developing such technologies—has been a great source of happiness and pride for me. I take satisfaction in knowing that I have been able to contribute, in my own way, to society through my work.

Over the years, I have had the privilege of spending time in both Japan and the United States, where I have worked with people of different environments, cultures, and languages. Despite these differences, we shared the same goal: to create products that would bring joy and value to people. When a project was completed, we shared the thrill of success together, and then moved on to the next challenge, starting a new development once again. I have been fortunate to spend many years gaining such invaluable experiences.

Working with people from various countries and backgrounds, I came to realize that it is human beings who both hurt and heal others. Yet I was fortunate to be surrounded by good colleagues within the organizations I belonged to, and through them, I was given countless opportunities to learn things that would enrich the value of my long life.

Through these experiences, I came to understand that for engineers to fully demonstrate their capabilities, it is essential to work in an environment built on mutual trust, clear and open communication, and genuine respect among team members. This foundation is critical for enabling engineers to perform at their best.

Having the basic technical skills is, of course, fundamental, but as mentioned, the team environment in which one works has an enormous influence on how effectively those abilities can be expressed. In a healthy environment of mutual respect, one can truly feel the power to generate new ideas and solutions beyond expectation. On the other hand, when working in an atmosphere of mistrust, it becomes difficult to produce meaningful results, both in quality and quantity, no matter how talented the individuals are.

Unfortunately, when Japanese and American engineers, each with their own cultural backgrounds and languages, work together, smooth communication can sometimes be difficult in reality. Misunderstandings occur, leading to incorrect conclusions, wasted time, and, at times, unresolved communication even after long hours of effort. Such situations are not only inefficient but also emotionally draining for both sides.

It has always saddened me to see people with the same goals, both striving for the best results, fall into conflict or confusion due to miscommunication. Beyond the sadness, I have often felt personal frustration that these unresolved conflicts and misunderstandings have taken up so much of my precious time. In today's environment, where development cycles must be ever shorter and efficiency is critical, there is no room for American and Japanese teams, both highly capable, to waste time because of avoidable misunderstandings.

However, I have also experienced that when people from these two different cultures intentionally rise to the challenge and succeed in creating a positive team environment, the power of such a hybrid team can become something truly extraordinary, which should be far beyond what either side could achieve alone.

It is easy to fall into conflict when mutual understanding is lacking. It is far more difficult to build the best team through mutual respect and genuine understanding. The choice of which path to take lies entirely with you.

That being said, isn't there tremendous value in embracing these challenges, working side by side with Japanese engineers, and building hybrid teams where each member brings out the best in the other? I believe that continuing to create such teams is not only possible, but essential for shaping the future of truly global engineering.

Introduction
Japan as a Critical Partner

For Japan, the United States is a truly special country. I would say because America has brought about *two miracles* in Japan's history.

The first occurred about 170 years ago, when Japan, the world of shoguns, samurai, and ninjas, was under a policy of limited diplomacy and was practically isolated from the rest of the world. The United States opened Japan's doors and introduced Western culture, setting off an extraordinary transformation. The second miracle came eighty years ago, when Japan surrendered to the Allied Forces at the end of World War II, yet was allowed to remain a sovereign nation.

In 1853, Commodore Matthew Calbraith Perry of the US Navy anchored four warships off the coast of Uraga, at the entrance of Tokyo Bay, and knocked on the doors of the Tokugawa shogunate. The resulting *Treaty of Peace and Amity* and later the *Treaty of Amity and Commerce* between Japan and the United States called for the opening of Japanese ports for trade. That was primarily to supply American whaling ships with fuel, food, and crew rest.

From Japan's point of view, some clauses, such as extraterritorial rights and the lack of tariff autonomy, were unequal. Yet, in contrast to European colonial expansion that often sought territorial control and opium trade, America's approach was markedly different. In hindsight, this first contact was nothing short of miraculous for Japan.

That encounter became the spark for Japan's modernization. Western clothing, cuisine, architecture, railways, postal systems, education, clocks, calendars, and gas lamps were eagerly adopted, transforming both society and daily life. This period became known as *Bunmei Kaika*—the "civilization and enlightenment" of Japan.

Japan's second great transformation came eighty years ago, when on September 2, 1945, Japan signed the *Instrument of Surrender* aboard the USS *Missouri,* anchored, by coincidence, in the same waters off Uraga coast where Perry's ships had once lain. Remarkably, the Allied Powers chose not to divide Japan under multiple occupations by the US, Soviet Union, China, and Britain, but instead entrusted the United States alone with governing and rebuilding Japan as a unified nation.

Over the course of several years, the United States helped Japan cast off militarism, totalitarianism, and ultranationalism, and guided the country through a revolutionary transformation. Eight decades ago, America introduced not only a new constitution but also such fundamental principles as popular sovereignty, separation of powers, gender equality, the dissolution of the *zaibatsu* conglomerates, land reform, educational reform, human rights, and freedom of speech.

Let me emphasize again that it was the United States, and no other country, that reshaped Japan twice. First by bringing Western culture, and later by helping establish the foundations of modern Japanese politics, economy, society, law, education, and culture.

For Japan, a country so profoundly transformed by America, the United States became a *big brother*—one whom the nation learned from, cooperated with, and walked alongside. This mindset continues to underlie Japan's political, economic, and business strategies today.

One clear example is Japan's approach to expanding into the American market. Take automobiles: rather than simply exporting right-hand-drive vehicles made for Japan, Japanese automakers designed and manufactured left-hand-drive cars from the very first unit (that happened to be the year I was born), ensuring that their products suited American lifestyles and preferences. When Japan's trade surplus and America's employment conditions became a concern, Japan responded by shifting production, supply chains, and even development bases to the US, focusing on transferring Japanese engineering and manufacturing expertise to American workers.

In other words, Japan has never viewed the United States merely as a market for profit, but as a *shared ground for growth*—a place to prosper together. Even though Japan faced concerns over the "hollowing out" of its domestic industries from the 1990s to the 2000s, and more recently the outflow of skilled engineers in the 2020s, there has been no move to restrict investment in or collaboration with the United States.

Let us look at the numbers. Japan is the largest foreign investor in the United States. Since 2019, including during the COVID-19 pandemic, Japan has held the top position every year. Japan's annual investments have increased by roughly $300 billion over the years. Total investment at the end of 2024 was $819.2 billion, ranking Japan first among all investor countries, ahead of Canada ($811.7 billion),

Germany ($677.3 billion), and the United Kingdom ($667.3 billion).[1]

Furthermore, Prime Minister Ishiba announced during his first in-person meeting with President Trump at the White House in February 2025 that Japan would raise its investment in the United States to **one trillion dollars**.[2]

Japanese companies continue to be the number one contributor to US merchandise exports among all US foreign investors since the late 1990s. That reached $82.3 billion in 2022. Japan's direct investment in the United States has provided well over two decades of significant US export growth, which has sustained American jobs and has increased the global competitiveness of the US economy.[3]

As Japan's capital investment in US manufacturing has increased, there has been substantial growth in the number of Americans employed by US-based Japanese manufacturers. In 2022, a record number of 529,200 Americans were employed by Japanese manufacturers in the US economy, the highest level among all foreign investors in the United States. Japanese investment in the US manufacturing sector has sustained American middle-class families for decades.[4]

---

[1] Jetro. "Japan's U.S. Investment Dynamic," 2023. https://www.jetro.go.jp/usa/japan-us-investment-report/.

[2] Ota, Akihisa, and Shinji Abe. "Ishiba Pledges to Boost Japan's Investment in U.S. To $1 Trillion; Trump Says Meeting with Nippon Steel..." *The Japan News*, February 8, 2025. https://japannews.yomiuri.co.jp/politics/politics-government/20250208-237666/.

[3] Bureau of Economic Analysis. "Activities of U.S. Affiliates of Foreign Multinational Enterprises, 2022 | U.S. Bureau of Economic Analysis (BEA)." *BEA,* 2022. https://www.bea.gov/news/2024/activities-us-affiliates-foreign-multinational-enterprises-2022.

[4] Jetro. "JAPAN'S U.S. INVESTMENT DYNAMIC." Jetro, 2025. https://www.jetro.go.jp/ext_images/usa/2025/Japan-US-Investment-Report/japans_us_investment_dynamics_2025_v2.pdf.

Historically, Japan has contributed numerous innovations to the world: the compact disc (CD), hybrid cars, pocket calculators, electronic dictionaries, lithium-ion batteries, QR codes, and maglev trains, to name a few. Today, Japan continues to drive advanced research and development. Working toward the realization of superconducting quantum computers exceeding 10,000 qubits, building supercomputing and AI infrastructure, and developing cutting-edge instruments for materials science, life sciences, and semiconductor research.

Japan is also advancing in regenerative medicine through iPS cell technologies, revolutionary drug development and production processes, and next-generation smart urban infrastructure that integrates AI, robotics, autonomous mobility, and smart homes. In environmental innovation, Japan leads in hydrogen energy, renewable energy, energy efficiency, and smart grids, with vigorous efforts toward achieving carbon neutrality by 2050.[5]

With such technological strength and aligned policy goals, Japan is unquestionably the most important partner with whom Americans should join hands in pursuit of a shared future.

Working with Japanese partners is not always easy. Their cultural background and ways of thinking differ greatly from those of the West. Yet the effort to understand Japan and its people yields immense rewards, because through that collaboration, it is possible to build engineering teams capable of *leading the world*.

---

[5] Ministry of Economy, Trade and Industry. "Green Growth Strategy through Achieving Carbon Neutrality in 2050 / METI Ministry of Economy, Trade and Industry." METI, October 17, 2022. https://www.meti.go.jp/english/policy/energy_environment/global_warming/ggs2050/index.html.

Just as America has long been special to Japan, Japan has now become a special nation for America as well. Understanding Japan, building partnerships with Japanese engineers, and working together as American engineers to lead the world are not only our responsibilities but also our privileges as professionals living in this era.

Part I

The Invisible Barrier—Understanding Culture

Chapter 1

The Engineer Torn Between Two Worlds

True strength is not in proving oneself right, but in admitting one is wrong.
—Author

Before we move into the main text of Part I, I would like to begin by revisiting a point I raised in the prologue: *It is easy to fall into conflict when mutual understanding is lacking.* Let's start with this idea. A few years ago, I encountered a situation that exemplified this very problem.

After finishing a business trip in Japan, I found myself at Narita Airport, folding my rain-soaked umbrella in the elevator and thinking, "At last, I can return to LA, where it never rains." Just then, two tall men behind me began talking.

One said quietly, "They didn't say yes or no." The other replied sharply, "They're hiding something. I don't trust them."

Suppressing a smile, I turned and said, "I'm sorry. It's none of my business but they're not hiding anything. They really just don't know whether it's yes or no."

The two men looked puzzled, as if wondering what on earth I was talking about. At that moment, the elevator doors opened onto the departures lobby and released us into the busy terminal.

There was no time to explain, but what stayed with me was that phrase: *"I don't trust them."*

Such a short-sighted statement and so devoid of thought or empathy. I couldn't help but feel sad. No doubt, those two would sit in a meeting with Japanese colleagues, fail to grasp what was happening, and conclude that they couldn't trust them either.

Understanding another person's perspective is never easy. Yet I am struck by how many people fail even to try.

Let's dive into the content. When Western engineers meet with Japanese engineers, the pattern often repeats. You, the Western engineer, have spent days preparing for the meeting. You present your findings with confidence, summarizing everything clearly. Then your Japanese counterpart says, "Thank you for the report. We'd like to consider this further and continue the discussion."

You're bewildered. *What more is there to consider?* No concrete questions, no specific feedback. The most senior Japanese engineer makes a vague comment that sounds half like agreement, half like hesitation. The others, who were supportive before the meeting, now remain silent. You wonder: *Are they in favor or against?* You can't tell.

You've answered every one of their questions even down to what you thought were unnecessary details, yet it's unclear whether they understood or are satisfied.

When you ask for a decision, they respond, "It's not so simple to say yes or no."

Deadlines loom, time slips away, and still there is no clear direction.

Between two worlds, Japanese and Western, you find yourself torn and frustrated, unable to do your best work as an engineer.

In your head, a voice mutters: *my explanation was perfectly clear. Working with Japanese people is just impossibly difficult.*

But is that really true? Are the Japanese the problem, or is there something else?

A wise engineer should pause and reflect.

To create, engineers need peace of mind. A calm, untroubled environment nurtures both mental and physical well-being, allowing ideas to flow freely.

The healthier the mind, the more creativity it generates. Maintaining this positive cycle is itself part of an engineer's job.

When you're in a good state, even if an experiment fails, you don't lose heart; you can simply move on to the next one.

Engineering is a gradual process of daily accumulation.

You work under pressure of deadlines, tight schedules, and high expectations, yet you must preserve and strengthen your creativity to see it through.

When stress builds, even knowing what needs to be done, you find yourself unable to start. You can't think clearly. You're no longer in a healthy state and your abilities decline. That's a *negative cycle.*

In such moments, it's tempting to blame others.

It's the Japanese who make everything so difficult.

Let's return to that phrase: *"I don't trust them."*

Have you ever said this about the Japanese you've worked with? If so, why?

That reaction comes from a deep instinct of the brain's primitive survival mechanism: *do not trust what you cannot understand.*

It's a function vital to survival. In evolution, creatures that failed to sense danger in the unfamiliar didn't leave many descendants. Those who avoided what they didn't understand survived. Therefore, that same instinct still lives in us.

But when people from different cultures and histories communicate, that instinct can hinder rather than help. To work together, we must *resist* the urge to retreat from the unfamiliar and instead engage our higher human faculties, that is the part of the brain capable of understanding.

It's not easy. Yet that effort to understand what you don't yet understand is essential.

When I first came to the US, I opened a bank account and received my very first checkbook.

A friend explained, "Here, even at the supermarket, people pay by check, not cash."

Indeed, thirty years ago, many shoppers would write checks at the register, showing their driver's license as ID.

That same friend also advised, "Always keep some cash in your pocket, in case you get held up by a robber." So one day I tried an ATM for the first time, planning to withdraw $40.

I inserted my card, pressed the "Fast Cash $40" button, and waited for two $20 bills.

What came out instead was a small slip of paper—slightly smaller than a check—printed with "Withdrawal: $40."

I thought for a moment and concluded, *"Ah, I see! This is a check-based country. The ATM must be issuing a $40 check."*

So I signed on the back of the slip and took it to the teller, saying, "Please cash this."

Naturally, the teller had no idea what I was talking about. After much back-and-forth, I was politely shown the door.

Later, I learned the ATM had simply run out of cash, and the receipt was printed by mistake.

Looking back, it was a perfect example of *cognitive bias,* the tendency to make illogical judgments based on assumptions, past experience, and intuition.

At the time, though, my reasoning seemed completely sound.

Let's digress briefly into cognitive psychology, because it sheds light on why cultural misunderstandings arise.

Our brains have a remarkable ability to *retrofit* reality, that is to adjust our memories after the fact so that they make sense.

I once heard a lecture at Caltech describing how, when you move your hand or finger, the brain actually sends the signal about half a second *before* you consciously decide to act.

Then, afterward, the brain inserts the feeling of "I decided to do that" into your memory.

Even when you clap your hands, the sight, the sound, and the tactile feeling all reach your brain at different times, yet the brain merges them into one "simultaneous" event.

In short, we're experts at constructing memories, even when they don't quite match reality.

I once experienced this firsthand.

Looking for some notes I had recorded, I flipped through my notebook. But the page I clearly remembered writing on was nowhere to be found.

I checked every similar notebook. Nothing.

I was certain I had written it down to the page position. It wasn't a dream.

I told myself repeatedly, *"It's there. I remember exactly."*

Days later, I discovered the truth: I had torn out the page and stored it elsewhere.

Yet I had completely forgotten doing so.

I had believed, with total conviction, in a false memory.

When you're convinced something is true, it never occurs to you that you might be wrong.

We've had arguments with friends or family: "You said that!" "No, I didn't!" "I'm not wrong!" "Yes, you are!"

Neither side is lying, just each is simply defending a memory their brain has faithfully constructed.

Even after being proven wrong, it's hard to accept.

Why mention this?

Because often, when we're "torn between two worlds" and find ourselves thinking, *"I'm right, the other side is wrong,"* we're reacting based on *constructed perceptions.* Not objective truth.

So in those moments, it helps to pause and think:

Wait... Maybe I'm mistaken.

Maybe there's something I don't yet know.

That small shift of perspective might be the key to resolving what seemed an impossible situation.

Japanese and Western engineers share the same goal: to do their best work and create something valuable.

When Western engineers feel "torn" in dealings with Japanese colleagues, it's rarely because the goals are misunderstood.

Rather, as the saying "lost in translation" suggests, both sides may be making the best decisions they can, yet find themselves lost then trapped by differing assumptions, or by their own unconscious biases.

To realize that *there are things you don't know you don't know*, to identify them, understand them, and integrate that knowledge into your thinking, that awareness can prevent you from ever being torn between two worlds again.

This book, based on my own experiences, aims to provide insights that will help American engineers work more effectively with their Japanese counterparts.

Departures Floor
...
I don't trust them.

Chapter 2
The Japanese Engineer's Mindset

Understanding others is never wrong;
it is always right.
—Author

Let us begin by looking back in time to explore how the Japanese engineer's mindset was shaped through history.

If someone asked, "What is the greatest difference between the West and the East?" how would you answer?

Whatever comes to mind is probably not far from the truth.

After all, when Western engineers think of the East, whatever words they may use, what they picture is, in many ways, precisely what defines it.

When I reflect on the differences between the Western and Eastern worlds, the first thing that comes to mind is this: in the West, the philosophies of Taoism, Confucianism, and Buddhism never truly took root.

These schools of thought originated mainly in present-day India and China. They spread westward as far as Gandhara, but there they seem to have been absorbed by Hellenistic culture and did not travel farther.

To the east, however, they crossed Tibet, China, and Korea, finally reaching Japan.

Conversely, Western thought that I assume to be from Hellenism and Byzantine culture was largely blocked, perhaps by the Khyber Pass, and never reached the Vedic lands of India or the civilizations to the east of it.

Thus, the philosophies that shaped Western civilization did not penetrate China, Korea, or Japan.

When these Eastern philosophies, such as Taoism, Confucianism, and Buddhism, eventually reached Japan, they brought ideas that can be summarized as follows:

Taoism teaches unity with nature and harmony with its flow:

"Live peacefully according to nature."

"Be flexible and humble like water."

"Never flaunt strength or wisdom."

"Abandon endless desire and avoid dissipating energy in conflict with others."

It is a philosophy of balance, of aligning one's life with the natural order.

Confucianism, on the other hand, emphasizes rules and discipline:

Courtesy, obligation, diligence, morality, integrity, dignity, virtue, and uniformity.

It provides the moral and social framework for living properly within a structured society.

Buddhism teaches salvation through spiritual enlightenment to extinguish desire, remove illusion, and attain peace of mind through realizing universal truth.

Around fifteen centuries ago, when the early Yamato court was forming what would become the nation of Japan, Confucianism was adopted as a system of order and governance, while Taoism and Buddhism were accepted as guiding philosophies.

Together they became the intellectual foundation of the emerging Ritsuryō *system,* the ancient Japanese legal code and the moral architecture of the nation.

Roughly 1,400 years ago, Prince Umayado—better known as Prince Shōtoku, the second son of Emperor Yōmei—established the *Seventeen-Article Constitution,* seeking to create a centralized state under imperial rule.[6]

Although it served as a moral and administrative code for officials, it also laid the groundwork for Japan's national ethos, influencing its politics and culture for centuries.

Among its seventeen articles are the following:

- **Article 1:** "Harmony should be valued, and an avoidance of wanton opposition to be honored."
- **Article 8:** "Let the ministers and functionaries attend the court early in the morning, and retire late."
- **Article 15:** "To turn away from that which is private, and to set our faces towards that which is public."
- **Article 17:** "Decisions on important matters should not be made by one person alone. They should be discussed with many."

What I find remarkable is that these principles, written 1,400 years ago as national law, mirror the very attitudes and behaviors we see in Japanese engineers today.

It is astonishing, yet entirely logical: Japan has carried these philosophies in its cultural bloodstream ever since.

---

[6] Aston, William George. *The Nihongi: Chronicles of Japan from the Earliest Times to A.D. 697,* 2013. https://novaonline.nvcc.edu/eli/evans/HIS111/Documents/JapCon.pdf.

For over a thousand years, from about 1,400 to 400 years ago, Japan was governed under a strong Ritsuryō system, a system of strong centralized control by emperors and military rulers.

Then, for roughly 250 years more (until about 150 years ago), the shogunate maintained similar centralized control during the era of strong, limited diplomacy.

During that long millennium, Japan's population remained relatively stable, and as an island nation, it saw little influx of foreign ideas or cultures.

This created a remarkably consistent environment for passing down the same modes of thought from generation to generation.

In such an environment, those who conformed to authority survived, while those who rebelled often perished.

Over time, obedience became a survival trait, which is then transmitted biologically through descendants and culturally through education.

Those who thought differently or voiced unorthodox ideas were branded as dangerous, often ordered to commit *seppuku* (ritual suicide), taking their families down with them through the system of collective punishment.

Thus, conformity, which was created from respect for Taoist and Confucian ideals, became embedded not only in social norms but, one might say metaphorically, in the nation's DNA.

In Richard Dawkins' terms, the *memes* of these philosophies were faithfully passed down through the centuries.

In the last 150 years, however, Japan's population exploded from roughly thirty million to over one hundred million.

With that expansion, one might expect new and diverse ideas to spread.

Yet, in generational terms, 150 years is only about five generations, a brief moment in the long span of cultural transmission.

I grew up being told by my mother and grandmother, *"Finish everything on your plate."*

Now I find myself saying the same words to my own children.

That simple observation proves, at least to me, how persistent certain ways of thinking can be.

Even in a rapidly expanding society, values can remain unchanged for many generations.

Thus, the philosophies born 1,400 years ago continue to live quietly within the Japanese mindset today.

Taoist philosophy teaches that all things are interconnected, that opposites—*yin* and *yang* complement each other to form a unified whole.

Like the *taijitu* symbol seen on the Korean flag, it holds that the black contains the seed of white, and the white, the seed of black.

Within *yes* lies *no*, and within *no* lies *yes*.

Nothing exists independently; everything in the universe is interrelated.

This worldview has deeply influenced Japanese thought, instilling a sensitivity to relationships and balance.

Confucianism, meanwhile, reinforces obedience to rules, respect for harmony, and sincerity in dealing with others.

As Japanese history shows, deviation from accepted norms was often treated as dangerous. Something to be eliminated for the sake of social order.

Some of the Western visitors in the past were struck by what they found.

Francis Xavier on the Japanese, writing to the Jesuits at Goa from Kagoshima, Japan, on November 5, 1549:

> *The people whom we have met so far are the best who have yet been discovered, and it seems to me that we shall never find among heathens another race to equal the Japanese. It is a people of very good manners, good in general, and not malicious; they are men of honor to a marvel, and prize honor above all else in the world.*[7]

Carl Peter Thunberg, a Swedish naturalist and disciple of Carl Linnaeus, recorded similar impressions during his travels in the eighteenth century:

> *The Japanese are respectful and friendly. They obey their rules strictly and subordinate themselves to superiors.*[8]

[7] Boxer, Charles Ralph. *The Christian Century in Japan, 1549-1650,* 1951.
[8] Kijewski, Leonie. "The Japanese Character and Its Peculiarity – A Study of Carl Peter Thunberg's Travel Account." MaRBLe, July 1, 2014. https://doi.org/10.26481/marble.2014.v6.223.

Such observations, "valuing honor," "being polite," "not stealing," "respecting authority," "obeying superiors," clearly reflected the long-standing influence of Taoist, Confucian, and Buddhist teachings on Japanese society.

Even today, Japanese people find harmony between the artificial and the natural, sensing interconnection in all things, believing that within *yes* lies *no* and within *no* lies *yes*.

They uphold discipline and order, seeing conformity to rules as a virtue, while dissent or deviation remains difficult to accept.

Most Japanese engineers embrace this social fabric instinctively, without conscious effort.

They are careful not to disturb the harmony around them, to act and speak in ways that preserve group balance.

I call this the "scrum effect."

In this environment, individuals willingly surrender a small part of their individuality to become part of a united team.

Within that collective, they find protection from personal risk, justification for their actions, and even a quiet sense of superiority.

It is a group consciousness born from unity, a way of surviving together by standing as one.

Many readers may have heard of the book, *Japan as Number One*, written by Harvard sociologist Ezra F. Vogel.

You may not have read it yourself, but if you ask Japanese people who lived through that era, most will say they have.

Published in 1979, the book was intended for American readers, urging them to understand Japan and learn from it.[9]

Ironically, it became a runaway bestseller not in the US, but in Japan. Half a million copies were sold in its first year.[10]

For many Japanese readers, the book's praise of Japan as a nation was felt personally as though recognition of the country itself meant recognition of the individual.

A sense of collective pride made it deeply satisfying for them.

Even today, we see echoes of that sentiment online.

Japanese social media is filled with posts celebrating how foreign visitors admire Japan's politeness and orderliness.

These self-affirming messages, often anonymous, sometimes exaggerated, serve as a way to strengthen collective pride, or the scrum effect.

As these examples illustrate, the Japanese generally prefer not to assert their own strengths themselves; instead, they would rather have those qualities recognized and praised by others.

Another legacy deeply woven into the Japanese spirit is reverence for *kami* (deities) and *buddhas*.

---

[9] Vogel, Ezra F. *Japan as Number One.* Harper Colophon Books, 1979.

[10] Wikipedia Contributors. "Japan as Number One: Lessons for America." Wikipedia, October 27, 2025.

Though distinct from Taoism, Confucianism, and Buddhism, this reverence lies at the root of Japan's imperial and national mythology.

The *Kojiki* (means "Records of Ancient Matters")[11] and *Nihon Shoki* (means "Chronicles of Japan")[12], both Japan's oldest chronicles, were written by the prince and the imperial commission and published in the early eighth century, and together they form the bedrock of Japanese mythology and early historiography, describing how the land itself came into being. As in many mythologies, the gods shape the world, but as anthropologist Claude Lévi-Strauss observed, Japan's mythology is unique in how it intertwines with *real history*.

He noted that Japan's myths and its political structures are inseparable. That history itself is rooted in mythic continuity. He called this blending of myth and history one of the most fascinating aspects of Japanese culture.[13]

Within these texts, we find deep reverence for tools and natural objects; in other words, echoes of gratitude toward the material world. From this springs the belief that "things have souls," that even inanimate objects possess *spirit*. This animistic worldview fostered the cultural ideal of *mottainai*—the ethic of not wasting, of treating objects with respect.

My mother and grandmother, who often told me *"Finish what's served,"* also said, *"Take care of things"* and *"Don't*

---

[11] Cartwright, Mark. "Kojiki." World History Encyclopedia, May 12, 2017. https://www.worldhistory.org/Kojiki/.

[12] Cartwright, Mark. "Nihon Shoki." World History Encyclopedia, May 16, 2017. https://www.worldhistory.org/Nihon_Shoki/.

[13] Lévi-Strauss, Claude. *The Other Face of the Moon.* Harvard University Press, 2013.

throw away what can still be used." Their words embody this inherited reverence for the material world.

It is no coincidence that Japanese engineers strive to create products that do not break easily, that are made to last, and that avoid waste. Behind that pursuit lies a deep cultural current, a worldview centuries old.

Japan may appear mysterious to outsiders. A "strange nation of strange people."

But the Japanese are not incomprehensible, nor are they impossible teammates.

Once mutual understanding deepens, you will find them to be among the most trustworthy and capable partners imaginable. That, I can assure you.

"Harmony should be valued, and an avoidance of wanton opposition to be honored."

"Let the ministers and functionaries attend the court early in the morning, and retire late."

"To turn away from that which is private, and to set our faces towards that which is public."

"Decisions on important matters should not be made by one person alone. They should be discussed with many."

Chapter 3
The American Engineer's Mindset

One must know oneself
before truly knowing another.
—Author

Now, what about Americans—those who have inherited the legacy of Western civilization? I believe that the patterns of thought and behavior found in modern Americans, who carry the cultural DNA of the West, can be traced all the way back to the Greek philosophy, rediscovered and re-evaluated during the Renaissance. Over time, through successive cultural movements such as the Reformation, the Enlightenment, and utilitarianism, this worldview evolved, transformed, and has been transmitted to the present day as a kind of cultural *meme*.

Europe's great flowering of culture arguably took place around the Renaissance or slightly before it. During that time, the *scholae*, which later developed into the medieval universities, emerged as centers of learning. Much like Japan's own early education systems, they originated some 1,400 years ago from religious instruction held in ancient Christian monasteries and cathedrals. Originally cathedral or monastic schools, they were gradually expanded, particularly during the Renaissance, by philosophers who incorporated elements of ancient Greek scholarship. These schools became places where debate and intellectual discourse were actively encouraged as essential components of learning.

It is easy to imagine that within those scholastic settings, philosophical discussions aimed at acquiring and interpreting knowledge like those said to have been pursued in Plato's Academy were encouraged, leading to lively exchanges of ideas. Likewise, the study of rhetoric and dialectic, promoted at Aristotle's Lyceum, would have spread and taken root there. In such environments of learning, discussions naturally extended to the natural sciences, directing people's attention toward understanding truth more deeply. Having mastered rhetoric and dialectic, individuals would have developed the ability to articulate what they believed to be true more clearly and persuasively, and then nurture a generation capable of influencing society through logic and reason.[14]

However, this inevitably gave rise to a latent conflict: that between free inquiry and the Church. The pursuit of natural science had the potential to touch upon domains that the Church might deem heretical and therefore seek to suppress.

It was in precisely such a context, I imagine, that Thomas Aquinas succeeded, guided by the principles of scholasticism, in avoiding open conflict with the Church. He seemed to embrace both Greek philosophy and the Christian faith, accepting each as a valid path to truth. Living in an era

[14] Spade, Paul Vincent. "Medieval Philosophy" In *Stanford Encyclopedia of Philosophy.*" Stanford University, 2004. https://plato.stanford.edu/entries/medieval-philosophy/.

where even a small misstep could lead to being branded a heretic, Aquinas did not remain silent. Instead, he labored to reconcile nature, reason, and faith, shaping his convictions into politically acceptable form and, through his own intellectual power, constructing a new social philosophy. That monumental work became *Summa Theologica*.[15]

Aquinas demonstrated the power of refining one's beliefs through rhetoric and dialectic, not to conform to existing society, but to transform it. His efforts showed that the individual could create new social thought rather than merely adapt to what already existed.

With *Summa Theologica*, the natural sciences came to be openly incorporated within the framework of religion, further strengthening religious society. And then there was Martin Luther. Although it may be difficult to say he was particularly skilled in dialectic, his use of rhetoric was masterful. By expressing his convictions in plain language, on posters and pamphlets that anyone could understand, he reached the masses.[16] Holding firm to his belief that one should not be content with the status quo, he acted in ways that resonated with the public. Without being crushed by the powerful established Church, he gave birth to Protestantism.

Thus, European society evolved through a history of repeatedly producing new ideas and social movements, each driven by individuals with the strength to bring them into being.

---

[15] Castaldy, Daniel. "Summa Theologica by Thomas Aquinas." EBSCO Information Services, 2023. https://www.ebsco.com/research-starters/history/summa-theologica-thomas-aquinas.

[16] Britannica. "Ninety-Five Theses | Work by Luther." In *Encyclopædia Britannica*, October 24, 2018. https://www.britannica.com/event/Ninety-five-Theses.

At the same time, Europe's history was one of constant turbulence: wars of conquest, religious wars, witch hunts, and the ceaseless mixing of different peoples. Whether they wished it or not, Europeans lived in an environment that never allowed prolonged stability. To survive, one needed the ability to convince ever-changing powers that one was not an enemy of the majority, each time.

Japan, too, had its age of warring states, where alliances and betrayals were part of politics. But such maneuvering was largely limited to the level of feudal lords. In Europe, however, ordinary citizens had to develop that same political and rhetorical skill for their own survival.

It became second nature to distrust strangers first, and when asked "Whose side are you on?" one needed the ability to deflect and navigate such questions skillfully, so as not to be branded a heretic. Through generations of such experiences, people inherited the verbal dexterity and social agility necessary to survive.

Thus, honing one's caution, rather than easily trusting others, became an essential survival skill, cultivated and refined over centuries. Perhaps it is this cultural background that makes modern Japanese sometimes feel, "They sure know how to talk," when describing Westerners.

As Europe moved into the modern era, thinkers such as John Locke and Jean-Jacques Rousseau emerged, proclaiming ideas like: *"Do not seek happiness in what already exists in society or institutions created by others. Happiness is something you must build yourself."*; *"All men are born with natural rights to freedom."*; and *"Political power exists to represent the people and to safeguard their rights."* Once again, we see a consistent emphasis on individual power and the respect for personal opinion within society.

Later, utilitarianism extended this humanistic philosophy even further. Thinkers like Jeremy Bentham and John Stuart Mill proposed that *"if an action brings about the greatest good for society, then it should be regarded as right,"* and *"the best choice is the one that produces happiness for the greatest number."* Such ideas have been widely embraced in Western societies and continue to hold influence even today.

By looking back over the history of Western social thought, we can clearly see how deeply individual rights, happiness, and expression have been valued. Just as Japanese social thought was shaped through long centuries of development, so too Western philosophy and culture were painstakingly built over generations, then forming the foundation of the modern American engineer's mindset.

It is important to understand, however, that the Western respect for individual opinion and action does not equate to selfishness or indulgence. Rather, it implies that each individual has an obligation to contribute to society through their own words and deeds. In Western culture, organizations do not exist to protect individuals; rather, they are entities that individuals themselves must uphold and protect. In that sense, utilitarianism can be understood as the activity of striving to create a better society.

Even if most Americans never consciously think about it, these values are deeply embedded in their behavior. For instance, in the US college admissions process, community involvement, volunteer work, club participation, and internship experience are given weight equal to academic achievement. Applicants are also required to submit essays describing their values, experiences, and goals that demonstrate how they can contribute to society. In Japan, by contrast, university selection tends to focus on academic performance.

Similarly, public demonstrations in America are not viewed as self-serving protests, but as collective expressions of people who feel a need to improve their communities. Participants know that protests alone will not solve everything, yet they act out of a sense of personal responsibility to contribute no matter whether consciously or not. What may appear as self-assertive behavior is, in fact, supported by a long cultural tradition in which individuals make their value known as a means of contributing to society and the organizations they belong to.

That said, I cannot help adding a slightly mischievous personal observation: There are times when I encounter people who justify their actions with an argument such as, *"My behavior is right because it ultimately benefits society."* These individuals use utilitarianism as a shield to validate their every word and deed. This, however, is something entirely different from what I have been describing here, and something we should all be wary of.

Given that we Americans have inherited a Western cultural tradition that values an individual's capacity to contribute to society, it should now be clear that our words and actions may not be properly understood or may even be misunderstood by Japanese people, who come from an Eastern cultural background that places greater importance on consensus rather than individual agency. Needless to say, being keenly aware of this point is essential when working together as a team with Japanese colleagues.

Things that exclude "artificial" from universe are "nature."

Chapter 4
Unexpected Similarities Between Americans and Japanese

Opposites in appearance, alike in essence?
—Author

Although having examined the cultural differences and the historical contexts that shaped them, I have also come to realize, through living in both societies, that beneath the surface of the many distinctions between the East and West, there flows a surprising current of shared values. Recognizing these similarities allows us to avoid unnecessary friction, to act and think in ways that both sides find natural and comfortable, and to foster mutual understanding especially when working together as a team with Japanese engineers.

The first area where the hearts of Americans and Japanese seem to resonate is in their work ethic. It is often said that Japanese people willingly work long hours, accepting weekend work as part of their responsibility when needed. Many would agree with this observation. In contrast, Americans are sometimes portrayed as ending their work precisely at closing time and switching completely into personal mode afterward. While this difference in approach is often emphasized, my own experience tells a different story. I have seen many Americans who value their professional duties deeply as they stay late or work on weekends when necessary. Their sense of professionalism and dedication to completing the job is remarkably similar to that of the Japanese. In this respect, the two are far more alike than different.

Another striking similarity lies in the concept of teamwork. Both Americans and Japanese, once they form a team, share a strong determination to achieve results together. They both understand that the success of the team directly translates into the success of the organization.

Although I had often sensed, through my own professional experience, how deeply Americans value teamwork, I had assumed that this was merely a characteristic unique to the Japanese-affiliated company I worked for. However, when I later had the opportunity to participate in a corporate training program conducted by a third-party organization, I came to understand that this emphasis on teamwork is, in fact, one of the essential elements of American management.

In that American management training program, a great deal of time was devoted to exercises that required participants to work not as individuals but as teams, offering practical approaches to problem-solving and mutual support. This was almost identical to the employee training I had received in Japan. I witnessed the emphasis on collaboration, shared goals, and collective responsibility binds both cultures closely together.

A sense of fairness is another moral compass that both societies share. True, their motivations may differ slightly.

Japanese culture tends to view fairness as a way to maintain harmony among people, while American culture regards fairness as a mark of personal integrity and trustworthiness. Yet, in both contexts, the ideals of *equal opportunity*, *transparency*, *honesty*, and *trust* are highly valued. Both cultures recognize that respect cannot exist where fairness is absent. Fairness, in essence, is the foundation of respect. This, too, is something I have come to grasp with certainty through my many years of living locally in the United States, and I can state without hesitation that it is true.

Closely related to teamwork is the notion of individualism in American culture. It is often misunderstood as self-centeredness, but in truth, it is rooted in the idea of individuals who can contribute to society while supporting one another. In that sense, it aligns deeply with the Japanese principle of harmony and mutual consideration. Both societies recognize that human connection is the very foundation of community life. In such environments, courtesy and respect naturally emerge as essential virtues. Expressions of gratitude, both in words and actions, form an integral part of social interaction. In Japan, this spirit takes the shape of customs such as *ochūgen*—midyear gift to superiors, colleagues, clients, teachers, doctors, or friends, to thank people who have supported you during the first half of the year— and *oseibo,* year-end gift offered to similar recipients to show appreciation for help and kindness received throughout the year and to strengthen ties ahead of the New Year. This spirit is also reflected in *nengajō,* New Year's greeting cards. In America, it is reflected in the widespread habit of sending thank-you cards on numerous occasions throughout the year. Though the customs differ, the sentiment of gratitude is shared.

Most importantly, both Japan and the United States are nations exceptionally blessed with respect for individual rights and personal freedom. It would not be an exaggeration to say that both societies are among the most fortunate in this regard. In the *Spider-Man* films, the hero's uncle famously says, "With great power comes great responsibility." I would rephrase that to say: "Freedom, a sacred human right, comes with responsibility." In Japan, there is an unspoken understanding that "freedom exists within the bounds of not causing trouble for others." Americans, on the other hand, tend to speak of *rights*, while Japanese people speak of *consideration*. Yet both perspectives share the same essence. That means that true freedom can exist only when it is accompanied by respect for others.

Despite the clear cultural differences between Japanese and Americans, both societies share a larger view: that individuals should strive not only for personal benefit but for the sustenance and advancement of society as a whole. Both cultures honor and nurture this ideal. That is precisely why Americans and Japanese are able to understand, complement, and respect each other. They find in their partnership not only cooperation, but a genuine resonance of shared humanity.

Chapter 5

Why Saying "No" Isn't Always No

If you seek a yes,
begin by making sure it isn't a no.
—Author

I am fully aware of how extremely difficult it is for anyone to use another person's native language with the same fluency and naturalness as their own. Yet, without somehow finding a way to communicate in a mutually understandable language, it would be nearly impossible for engineers to even begin their work together. For that reason, in most cases, it is the Japanese side who courageously attempts to communicate in somewhat uncertain English when speaking with American colleagues.

Whether it is because the Japanese dictionaries are inaccurate, or perhaps because somewhere along the way English has been taught to Japanese people in a slightly misleading manner, I do not know. But for some reason, there are certain English expressions that many Japanese people tend to use with the wrong nuance.

For example, when they mean to say "I'm working on this project," they might say, *"I'm in charge of this project,"* which actually implies they are the leader or the one with authority. Or, intending to say *"I'm confident in my idea,"* they might instead say *"I have confidence in my idea."* Likewise, the expressions *"Let's discuss it"* and *"Let's talk about it"* somehow get mixed together and become *"Let's discuss about it."*

There are also cases where Japanese speakers, without any intention of sounding commanding, end up saying things like *"Please check it"* or *"I mean it,"* which to American ears can sound overly strong or even bossy.

When asking American colleagues casually to help them with English, some Japanese might say *"Please teach me English,"* which, in nuance, sounds like *"Please give me formal lessons in school."* Similarly, I occasionally see Japanese people say *"I'm very interesting,"* when they mean to say *"I'm very interested."*

I myself once used *"behind"* with an *"a"* in front of it by mistake, and later turned bright red when I realized what I had said.

When Japanese people are trying their best to communicate in English, and you notice that something sounds a little off, I believe the right thing to do is not to ignore it but to gently check the nuance or help correct the usage. For instance, if a Japanese person says *"I mean it"* in a situation that is not an argument or a heated debate, rather than getting offended, it would be far better to tell them that the expression doesn't quite fit that context.

Because languages are deeply rooted in culture, we must recognize that they carry delicate shades of meaning, and that errors in translation or interpretation are bound to occur from time to time.

One area that is particularly challenging for Japanese speakers is the type of question where a *"no"* answer is expected. Questions like *"Do you mind?"* or *"Don't you mind?"* For example, when asked whether a seat is available, many Japanese instinctively answer *"Yes"* because in their minds they are translating it as "Yes, please (go ahead)." I too, have sometimes found myself momentarily confused when, in the middle of a conversation, someone suddenly asks, *"Don't you think so?"*

Through many such experiences, I have learned that, as a non-native speaker of English, it is often better not to rely solely on *"yes"* or *"no"* responses, but to respond with the actual content of what I mean. For instance, when asked, *"Don't you mind if I take the seat?"* I, try not to answer simply *"yes"* or *"no,"* but instead say something like, *"I don't use this seat,"* which conveys the intended meaning more clearly.

Listening carefully to conversations among Americans themselves, I've also noticed that even native speakers sometimes need to confirm what *"yes"* or *"no"* actually means in a given exchange. It seems that even between native speakers, those two words alone are not always enough to ensure mutual understanding.

And how does this play out in the workplace?

When your superior says "no," it usually means the matter is closed. You can't push it any further. I remember once going to my boss's office after being told "no," hoping to make one more attempt. He looked at me and said firmly, "You know how to spell 'no,' right? N-O." That was the end of the conversation.

Among Western engineers, both the one who says "no" and the one who receives it understand that the discussion ends there. The person making the decision is expected to make a clear, responsible judgment on behalf of the organization, and once that decision is rendered, it's regarded as final.

In Japan, however, things are not always so absolute. Of course, there are cases where "no" really does mean "no," and the matter is closed. But not every "no" falls into that category. To many American engineers, this may seem puzzling, but in Japan, there are "no" responses that do not close the case. Some "no," in fact, contain a "yes" within them.

So, when you are told "no," your first task is to determine whether it is a completely black "no" as a final decision, or a gray "no," one that may still allow for further discussion. Because there are different shades of "no," even the person who said it often wants to be sure their true intent has been correctly understood. Therefore, after receiving a "no," it's wise to confirm what that "no" really means. If you approach this clarification respectfully and with good manners, the other person will usually respond favorably.

That said, directly asking "Was that a black no or a gray no?" would likely offend them. Instead, you might say something like:

"Thank you very much for taking the time to consider this matter. I understand your response regarding this issue. However, since this may affect future discussions, may I just confirm one thing?"

Then continue with:

"I believe we're both aiming for the same broader goal, and I want to make sure there's no misunderstanding about that. Am I correct?"

If the other person replies, "Well, yes, that's true," then you've successfully drawn out the "yes" hidden within the "no." That small acknowledgment gives you an opening to keep the discussion alive, avoiding a complete case closure.

If you succeed in doing that, the next step is to show humility:

"In that case, I suppose there must be a valid reason why my proposal wasn't acceptable. I realize my explanation may have been inadequate. My apologies for that."

By admitting your proposal may have been insufficient, you show respect. Yet even as you do so, you should begin thinking silently, *"If I can fill those gaps, I might remove the reasons behind the no."* Of course, you can't ask outright what those gaps are. You must figure them out yourself. To do that, it helps to understand the typical reasons behind a Japanese "no."

---

1. Testing Your Conviction

One common reason is that the "no" is actually a test of how serious you are. In other words: *"If you back down after being told no once, then that's the real reason for the no."*

The person may be checking your persistence and belief in your proposal. If you are confident in your idea, you must show that you won't give up easily. In such a case, you can respond by saying:

"I understand your response today. However, since we share the same goal, may I take some time to reconsider and return later to explain once more?"

The Japanese side will likely respond, "All right, please do that."

2. Lack of Precedent

Another possible reason is the lack of precedent. The idea may sound reasonable, but if it has never been done before, people are reluctant to say "yes" easily. As I will discuss in the chapter on processes, when there is no prior example, the standard procedures for judgment are unclear, and that makes decision-making itself difficult.

In such a case, you could propose:

"It's true that a first attempt is difficult to approve since there's no past example to follow. So how about this: we proceed a little, and if it doesn't work, we stop right away."

Then outline a step-by-step plan, setting clear goals for each phase: if the target of Step 1 is achieved, move to Step 2; if not, stop there. Present Steps 2 and 3 in the same structured way, adding:

"We'll move forward carefully, step by step, but if you ever have concerns, we'll stop immediately."

By making it clear that the Japanese side retains full control, they will likely respond, "All right, let's try it gradually."

3. Insufficient Consideration of Risks

A third reason may be insufficient attention to risks. When proposing a project, people naturally tend to emphasize its advantages. But the more enthusiastically you insist that your idea is correct, the more anxious your Japanese counterparts may feel. They begin to wonder, *"What's the catch?"*

If the risks are unclear, they hesitate to say yes. As I will mention in the chapters on report writing and presentation, when making a proposal, it's best to balance your description of benefits with an equal focus on potential concerns and risks.

If you suspect that the "no" you received was due to inadequate risk analysis, you might say:

"You're right, our list of potential risks and corresponding countermeasures was insufficient. May I take some time to review this important aspect carefully and come back to explain it again?"

The Japanese side will likely say, "Yes, please do that."

4. Lack of Consensus

Sometimes the "no" is simply because sufficient consensus has not yet been reached. The technical explanation may be clear, and there may be no objections in principle, but the necessary agreement among departments has not been obtained.

In Japan, reaching consensus among the relevant departments before a decision is important. When the views of related members or departments are not fully aligned, getting a "yes" can be difficult. Ideally you would secure all necessary approvals from all the relevant departments beforehand.

If you sense this may be the issue, you could ask:

"Would it be better to broaden the range of departments involved in supporting this proposal?"

"Which departments would you consider particularly important?"

These kinds of questions help you gain insight into the internal alignment process.

In most cases, these are among the reasons behind a "no." By respecting the thinking behind it and seeking ways to contribute through your proposal, you can often find a path forward.

A Case in Point: The Hydrogen Fuel Cell Truck

On April 17, 2017, in one corner of the Port of Los Angeles, where more than 15,000 heavy-duty trucks with fifteen-liter diesel engines come and go each day, a truck that emitted absolutely no exhaust gas made its debut. It was the world's first hydrogen fuel cell truck developed by a major Japanese automaker as an OEM demonstration vehicle.

I was fortunate to serve as the local project leader for its development. For the Port of Los Angeles, striving to reduce emissions, the launch of this zero-emission demonstration truck was of great symbolic importance. Yet behind this remarkable achievement, completing the project in just one year, was a success story born from the perfect harmony between Japan's strong technical development methodology and the expertise of US local companies responsible for the truck's production.

I recall that the decision to begin development was made in the summer of 2015. The project had a clear purpose: reducing diesel emissions, addressing port needs, and contributing to the community. However, even though its importance was recognized, it was an unprecedented technical challenge under a tight schedule, and obtaining consensus from the Japanese side required a careful approach.

Questions arose: could a thirty-six-ton truck really be powered by an electric motor? What if it broke down on the bridge inside the port? Understandably, the technical division could not easily give approval. Even for a prototype, causing disruption to truck drivers or container operators was unacceptable.

To gain the Japanese organization's agreement, I focused on three things:

1. Explaining in concrete terms how this project would contribute to the US business.
2. Identifying potential technical concerns and presenting countermeasures.
3. Establishing collaboration with a highly experienced and trustworthy local company with a proven track record in heavy-duty truck systems.

Through these efforts, I was able to present both the necessity of the project and the fact that we were fully aware of the potential risks and had measures in place to mitigate them. I made presentations to multiple departments including engineering, finance, and others and ultimately secured company approval.

Still, even that final decision was not an outright "yes." It was more along the lines of "We do not object, but please proceed with great caution," with the clear condition that if the plan did not progress as expected, we should not push forward.

There are many kinds of "no," as we have seen. In any case, once you are told "no," turning it into "yes" is never easy. Therefore, the smarter approach is to think ahead and avoid receiving a "no" in the first place.

It is unwise to press the Japanese side with questions like, "How can I make you say yes?", "What's wrong with my proposal?", or "Why can't you agree?" Reflect honestly. Have you ever taken that kind of approach yourself? If so, it's time to act more wisely.

Sharpen your sensitivity. When you sense hesitation, say instead:

"I understand that it may be difficult to say yes at this stage, but before deciding no, could we discuss together how we might make it possible?"

By taking that initiative, you remove the opportunity for the other person to say "no."

When you position yourself as someone not demanding a "yes," but as an ally helping the other person reach a decision, you'll earn their trust and confidence. If you can make them say, "Then please shape it into something I can say yes to," you've succeeded completely.

"No" spells
N-O.
Yeah... but it can still
have a "yes" inside.

Chapter 6

Process over Outcome: Why the Journey Matters in Japan

"It is what it is" sounds less like wisdom and more like surrender.
—Author

There's a movie starring Jim Carrey called *A Series of Unfortunate Events*. It's a funny film, but I found myself muttering that very title under my breath one night when I experienced a string of unfortunate events of my own.

My flight to Detroit was already badly delayed, and by the time I finally arrived, it was past midnight. Because of the delay, the rental car reservation I had made was canceled. After a long negotiation, the clerk finally managed to find a car for me, but when I got in, the battery was dead and the engine wouldn't start. I trudged back and forth across the frozen rental lot, under zero degrees Fahrenheit at two in the morning, until I was given a working vehicle. Exhausted, I finally reached the hotel, only to be told that my reservation wasn't in their system. The receptionist, smiling politely, said, "Please wait just a moment while I find another hotel nearby for you…" By then, it was already three in the morning. What happened after that, I'll leave to your imagination.

Mistakes happen, sometimes far too many at once, but they're dealt with, and once handled properly, the matter is considered resolved. That attitude comes from living in American society, and it reflects certain roots of Western culture itself.

Certainly, this view is my own personal opinion, one that could be shaped by the unfortunate events to which I was exposed and the hardships they brought. However, it is not based on those experiences alone. It is also the conclusion I have reached through what I learned in classrooms over the years, as well as what I have actually experienced in both Japanese and American societies. While it remains a personal perspective and may not earn everyone's agreement, I would like to outline below the thinking from which this view originates.

America is a nation built by immigrants with a history of frontier exploration. It's a society that values challenge and risk-taking. Even failure is seen as part of learning, an inevitable, even necessary, step toward success. The culture of "second chances" has deep religious and moral foundations: in church, anyone can confess their sins and be forgiven if they truly repent. The emphasis lies not on the sin itself, but on how one corrects it and grows afterward. This mindset, focusing on *quick recovery* rather than *prevention at all costs,* may well be one reason why Americans place such value on swift corrective action.

Japan, by contrast, has long valued harmony and order above all else, as symbolized by Prince Shōtoku's *Seventeen-Article Constitution*, as mentioned in Chapter 2, which states, "Harmony should be valued." I believe this thought was also well aligned, therefore nurtured by Japanese society, it grew from agricultural communities where individual mistakes could cause trouble for the entire group. As a result, *avoiding failure* became a survival strategy.

As I will mention again in later chapters, Japan's "culture of shame" means that failure can lead to a loss of social trust and standing. Consequently, people learn to place great importance on careful preparation and advance confirmation, and these become habits deeply ingrained not only in individuals but in the structure of society itself.

During Japan's feudal Edo period, social order was maintained through strict hierarchies and systems that discouraged error. Experienced masters trained newcomers according to established norms, and when mistakes occurred, collective responsibility systems ensured accountability. In such a world, free experimentation or trial-and-error challenges were rarely permitted. In this sense, Japan's culture stands as the complete opposite to America's frontier spirit.

Both historical paths still influence their modern societies. In Japan, being "someone who doesn't make mistakes" is often equated with competence. This mindset tends to suppress bold challenges and experimentation. In the United States, by contrast, "fail fast, learn fast" has become a mantra of innovation, driving the rise of startup culture and the spirit of risk-taking.

Because Japan is a society that fundamentally does not *assume* mistakes will occur, it is also a society that finds *responding* to mistakes particularly difficult.

I remember once at Narita Airport, I bought a toy, but moments later I saw another toy right next to it that I preferred. So I told the same clerk, "I'd like to return this one and buy that one instead. I'll pay the price difference." The clerk replied politely, "Was there anything wrong with the product?" I said, "No." She then said, "I'm sorry, but we cannot accept returns in that case." I protested, "But I just bought it from you a minute ago!" The clerk, still smiling, replied, "Yes, but as you have already made the purchase, I'm afraid we cannot accept a return." By this time, other customers were staring at me. What struck me most was how impeccably courteous the clerk remained throughout the entire exchange.

Statistics show that Amazon's return rate in the US is between 5 and 15 percent. Though I must admit, I'm one of those who contribute to that 5 and 15 percent. According to the study, the US industrywide average e-commerce return rate is about 17 percent. Sixty percent of the returns are due to fit or quality issues and 30 percent of returns come from customers changing their minds.[17] When I see numbers like this, I think, whether the mistake is in customers' or the e-commerce's, the system is designed to *assume* mistakes will happen. Because of that, returns and exchanges, which serve as "after treatment," are incredibly simple. I believe this "error-tolerant" system is well adapted to American society.

---

[17] Red Stag Fulfillment. "How many Amazon orders get returned each year? (2025 data)" *Red Stag Fulfillment,* May 19, 2025. https://redstagfulfillment.com/how-many-amazon-orders-get-returned/.

On the other hand, I could not even find any official nationwide refund/return rate study report that is published in Japan. This may be one piece of evidence that Japan has no interest in returning the items. One of the reports says "Japan's approach to returns is very different from Western norms.[18] No law requires merchants to accept returns for a change of mind. Returns are purely a courtesy or a contractual term set by each seller." This statement matches exactly with my own experience.

I've personally had three cases where checks not meant for me were mistakenly deposited into my account. At the time I was not only amazed but also in disbelief. While that was shocking at first, I was equally surprised by how quickly and smoothly the errors were corrected.

At restaurants in Japan, servers don't usually come back to the table to check whether your order was correct. That seemed normal to me until I moved to the US. I was quite surprised at first when servers repeatedly came by to ask if everything was right with my meal.

In Japan, mistakes are not just individual missteps. They are perceived as disruptions of social harmony and trust. This idea is deeply ingrained from childhood. In elementary school, as I remember and felt it, teachers emphasized giving the *correct* answer, and students avoided speaking unless they were one 100 percent sure. The unspoken message from teachers was clear: making mistakes is bad.

[18] E-housing. "Internet Shopping in Japan: Best Sites, Delivery, and Return Policies | E-Housing." *E-housing,* August 2, 2025. https://e-housing.jp/post/internet-shopping-in-japan-best-sites-delivery-and-return-policies.

From my experience, when an error occurs in the US, people move quickly to fix it. They don't dwell on *why* it happened; instead, they focus on the *best possible immediate response* and then close the case. In Japan, however, the emphasis is on tracing the cause, ensuring it never happens again, and codifying that prevention into new rules. The case remains open until the root cause is fully understood and shared. The focus is collective: analyzing the mistake to make sure no one repeats it.

Neither approach is right nor wrong. They're simply different philosophies of response.

Because mistakes are to be avoided, Japanese people hesitate to make quick yes-or-no decisions. Americans, by contrast, think, "If something goes wrong, we'll fix it," so they are more comfortable making clear decisions. The difference in how each culture *views* error influences how each decides.

As mentioned in the previous chapter, Japanese thinking often follows a "scrum" mindset, that everything is interconnected, and one issue affects many others. When an error occurs, its ripple effects spread across multiple departments. The relevant teams then gather to analyze: *why did it happen? Could similar issues arise elsewhere? How serious is it? Is it spreading? What is the potential impact?* The group surrounds the problem, as ants might swarm a candy dropped in the mud, covering it completely until it dissolves and disappears. Only then is the issue considered resolved, and the resulting lessons are distilled into a new *standard process* to prevent recurrence.

There's a proverb, *"Can't see the forest for the trees."* It describes someone so focused on one detail that they miss the big picture. But in engineering, the reverse can be just as dangerous. Of course, correct overall results are important, but understanding the fine details that led to those results is even more crucial. One must analyze not only *what* worked but *why* it worked, and whether hidden risks might emerge under different conditions. Ignoring the process of the journey that led to success can cause future problems to be overlooked. That's easier said than done, of course.

Standardized processes are powerful tools born from long experience and countless trials, not labeled as "failures," but as steps of learning. Following these processes reduces the need to recheck every detail each time, while also eliminating many potential causes of error.

Imagine a thriving forest of lush, healthy trees. From a distance, it looks vibrant. But if one tree becomes sick, that problem could spread through the entire forest. By studying the cause, such as sunlight, fertilizer, and water, you can discover the conditions for healthy growth. Once those are found, applying them to every tree ensures the whole forest thrives. In this analogy, carefully analyzing the one "sick tree" leads to a *standard process* that raises the quality of the entire forest.

Even if the person responsible for watering or fertilizing changes, as long as everyone follows the same process, the forest's quality remains stable. And if you plant a new forest, you can rely on the same established process to avoid repeating old mistakes.

For Japanese engineers who strive to avoid mistakes, this focus on process is deeply meaningful. When a problem occurs, they not only fix it, but they also investigate its cause and spend considerable time developing a process to prevent recurrence. These processes become a kind of sacred text that is comprehensive, time-tested, and not easily altered. The reverence for process has deep historical roots, and it deserves respect.

Even if someone climbs to the summit quickly, without following the proper process, their achievement isn't recognized. It might have gone well *this time*, but perhaps only because they happened not to fall into a crevasse by luck. Without tracing the standard route, their success remains unproven.

Yet here lies a paradox: engineering is, by nature, the pursuit of challenges that no one has ever attempted before. How, then, can you climb a mountain that no one has climbed, and still prove your success wasn't just a fluke?

The answer lies in updating existing processes with new information suited to the new challenge. There are two key points in doing so: first, understand the *intent* of the current process and carry it forward; second, add or modify conditions to reflect new realities.

For example, if the process once said, "After rain, do not step on tree roots," the intent was "to avoid slipping." If you are now climbing a rocky mountain with no trees, the updated process would be, "Do not step on wet rocks." That's an example of the first type of update. The second type occurs when technology itself changes. As if, say, new hiking boot soles are made of material that never slips, the "don't step on tree roots" rule should be deleted entirely.

There's an old European fable about a child whose mother once told him, "Butter melts in the heat, so wrap it in banana leaves and dip it in the river from time to time when carrying it." Later, when the child carried a kitten, he did the same—dipping it in the river, of course, with disastrous results. His mother then said, "At times like that, tie it with a string and pull it along." So when the child later carried a pot, he did exactly that, dragging it behind him and ruining it.

In engineering, similar situations can arise. For example, when designing for low-temperature performance, the quality of rubber, oil, and transistors has improved year by year. Yet if we continue to follow old processes that ignore such advances, we risk overdesigning unnecessarily, like the child misapplying outdated instructions.

Still, revising these "scriptures" of accumulated experience is extremely difficult. In complex control programs, even a small change can have unpredictable consequences, so engineers often hesitate to alter anything.

But unless new information is continuously incorporated, the standard process will lose its usefulness. And here is where American engineers can shine.

To truly harness the value of process, one must understand not only its visible form but its *intent*. By grasping the meaning behind each step, American engineers can help propose necessary updates and refinements. Those who respect the Japanese emphasis on process but can also view it from a different cultural angle are in a unique position to strengthen it.

After all, in technology development, achieving results quickly has great value. But it would be a mistake to criticize the process simply because it takes time. Instead, respect it, understand its value, its history, and where it can or cannot be revised.

My hope is that American engineers working with Japanese teams will become partners who support practical, living processes that honor tradition yet remain adaptable to new challenges.

Don't worry about the
result... if you followed
the recipe *process.*
Recipe

Chapter 7

Rules, Harmony, and the Boundaries of Individual Judgment

When the path is ignored, fortune masquerades as achievement.
—Author

In Japan, whenever an individual acts or speaks, they are expected to consider carefully the impact their behavior may have on those around them. At times, this consideration can seem excessive. As mentioned earlier in the section on how "no" doesn't always mean no, and as I will touch on again later, this tendency stems from a deeply rooted cultural emphasis on consensus.

When an individual makes a mistake or takes a risky action, there is rarely a clear mechanism for assigning personal responsibility. More often, the failure of one person is treated as the collective responsibility of the organization to which they belong.

The Japanese are particularly sensitive to the concept of *shame*. When someone behaves or speaks in a socially inappropriate way, they might be told, *"You'll bring shame upon yourself,"* or *"You should feel ashamed."* The word *shame* implies dishonor or loss of dignity. It's a warning not to invite ridicule or disgrace. Yet in Japanese, the unspoken subject of that warning is plural: it means not only "you will feel shame," but "you will make *all of us*, including yourself, feel shame." People understand this implicitly and thus take great care in what they say and do, striving not to inconvenience or embarrass those around them.

Decisions, therefore, are often made not from an individual perspective but according to the will of the organization. That is, by the standard of *what will prevent the organization from losing face.*

This reflects the same collective mindset described in the previous chapter. The belief that harmony leads to better outcomes and that the best conclusions arise through group deliberation. Yet adapting to such a social environment can have side effects: not only do individuals refrain from expressing personal opinions, but over time, some even stop forming opinions of their own.

Still, in Japan, keeping one's opinions to oneself doesn't put a person in a weaker position. On the contrary, by taking shelter within the safety of the group, individuals actually strengthen their social survival. Because responsibility is shared, the risk of being singled out for blame is low. Instead, accountability takes the form of *collective responsibility*, known in Japanese as *renza*—literally, being "chained together." Successes and failures alike belong not to individuals but to the group or society as a whole.

From my own experience, I often heard remarks like, "Can you take responsibility if that fails?" or "What will you do if it doesn't work?" But such words didn't mean, "You'll be personally responsible." What they really meant was, "You realize that if you fail, the group will be held accountable too, don't you?" In other words, I was being reminded that any decision I made that carried *renza* risk should first be discussed with, and approved by, the group.

To understand just how far-reaching this concept of shared responsibility can be in Japan, let me share a true historical example from about a century ago.

On December 27, 1923, when Emperor Shōwa was still Crown Prince, an assassination attempt was made on his life while he was traveling by car. Although the attempt failed, the mere occurrence of the event created a crisis of responsibility for the Japanese government. The result was astonishing: the entire Cabinet resigned; the Chief of Police and the Director of the Police Affairs Bureau were dismissed; the governor of the assailant's home prefecture was docked two months' pay; the governor of Kyoto Prefecture, which the assailant had visited the previous day, received a formal reprimand; and both the principal and the homeroom teacher of the elementary school the assailant had once attended resigned.[19]

This extreme case, though a hundred years old, vividly illustrates the breadth of *renza* in Japanese society. And it still echoes in modern Japan, even within the organizations where Japanese engineers work today.

Such a system, in which the organization guarantees responsibility, undeniably strengthens organizational cohesion. Yet to reduce the risks of *renza*, individuals must act only within boundaries formally sanctioned by their organizations. Rules, therefore, become crucial. Much like the

[19] Wikipedia Contributors. "Toranomon Incident." *Wikipedia*, January 23, 2025. https://en.wikipedia.org/wiki/Toranomon_incident.

emphasis on *process* described earlier, following officially approved rules allows individuals to avoid situations where they would have to bear personal blame, and it protects the organization from collective embarrassment. In such an environment, rules are not mere *guidelines.* They are treated as near absolutes.

You may have heard the expressions *"Do things right"* and *"Do the right things."* When people rely heavily on established rules, their behavior tends to align with *"Do things right."* This aligns closely with Confucian ideals such as propriety, duty, morality, sincerity, and harmony. By following prescribed norms, one avoids disturbing the order of the group and causing trouble for others. For Japanese engineers, this mindset, that is to entrust judgment to the rules, is not only natural but also encouraged.

Even in my own daily life, I catch myself hesitating before stepping onto a grassy area in a public park. I instinctively look for a sign that says whether it's allowed. Then I check what others are doing, trying to act the same way they do. I realize that while I'm quite good at recognizing rules and conforming to group behavior, I'm not very skilled at deciding for myself what's right based solely on the situation. In other words, *doing the right thing,* independent of written rules, doesn't come naturally to me.

Let me share a personal story that I experienced.

When the Y2K (year 2000) scare loomed, the fear that computers would crash at the turn of the millennium, I decided to put my faith in technology. On January 1, 2000 (Japan time), or December 31, 1999 (US time), I boarded a flight from Narita to Los Angeles.

Many people around me were genuinely worried about what might happen. But the contrarian in me whispered, *"Surely this will be the safest day to fly. Every airline will assign its most experienced pilots. Air traffic controllers worldwide will be on highest alert, prepared for power outages or system failures. The sky will be the safest place to be."* So, without hesitation, I booked the flight.

At the airport, after checking my large suitcase, I found myself with three carry-on items: a backpack, a paper shopping bag, and a Boston bag. After security, I arrived at the gate. The plane, a jumbo jet with over 400 seats, had perhaps thirty passengers in total with some, like me, confident in technology; others, traveling out of unavoidable necessity. It felt like boarding a small aircraft. I even wondered whether they would actually take off with so few on board.

Just as I reached the gate, the attendant approached me politely but firmly:

"Sir, I'm sorry, but each passenger is allowed only two carry-on items."

Her tone was impeccably courteous, but her eyes sparkled with quiet determination.

Surprised, I replied honestly, "Oh, but the flight's practically empty. There'll be plenty of overhead space, right?"

She smiled and said, "Yes, sir, I understand, but it could inconvenience other passengers, and we ask everyone to cooperate equally. We can't make an exception just for you."

I blinked. *Inconvenience other passengers?* I thought. Even if everyone brought ten bags, there would still be room to spare. What on earth was she talking about?

I tried again, still polite: "But as you can see, the plane is almost empty. Surely just one extra small bag…"

Before I could finish, she said crisply, "Yes, but those are the rules, sir. I'm afraid we can't allow you to board otherwise."

I mumbled to myself, "But that rule is meant to prevent crowding, and it doesn't really apply today…" At that point, three other attendants appeared, their eyes gentle but unyielding, making it clear the discussion was over.

So I went back into the terminal, bought a slightly larger shopping bag, stuffed my backpack and paper bag inside, and thus, although my single bag was now physically *larger,* I had successfully reduced my carry-ons to *two*.

When I returned, the attendant smiled and said, "Thank you for your understanding, sir. I'm sorry for the inconvenience, but rules are rules."

Once on board, I could have placed my bags ten meters away in any direction to front, back, or across the aisle. The cabin was nearly empty.

As someone born and raised in Japan, I can laugh about this story. But if you are an American, you must *not* laugh.

In the United States, however, the cultural baseline is entirely different. The phrase *"I am the rule"* captures it well. Americans generally do not see rules as sacred conclusions derived from collective wisdom. Instead, rules are seen as frameworks created to ensure that individuals from diverse backgrounds can coexist without unfairness or discomfort.

Because American society is built on diversity, people of different origins, values, and lifestyles, rules exist primarily to protect individual rights, not to enforce social uniformity. When someone violates a rule, that person alone is held accountable. Their group or organization does not share the punishment.

Moreover, in the US, personal judgment based on *doing the right thing* is respected even when it doesn't strictly follow the rules. If someone can explain the reasoning behind their decision and it's seen as *reasonable*, their action is often accepted. The very word *reasonable* captures this ethos; it implies logic, empathy, and fairness, not blind adherence.

Let's summarize it again here:

The difference lies in the social foundation. Japan is a society that values *uniformity*, where being alike ensures harmony and safety. People protect themselves by aligning with rules and staying in step with others.

In the US, diversity is valued, and individuals are encouraged to act according to their own judgment, protecting themselves through sound, independent decision-making.

Neither system is inherently superior. Each evolved as a survival strategy best suited to its own environment.

Ultimately, balance and understanding are what matter most. As the saying goes, *"When in Rome, do as the Romans do."* Acting according to local customs, armed with accurate knowledge and a sense of balance, smooths interactions in any situation.

For Japanese engineers working in the United States, following Japanese-style rules too rigidly will only make collaboration difficult. Likewise, for American engineers working with Japanese teams, taking the time to understand and respect Japan's cultural and social background will lead to far better results.

If you wish to work effectively and build a strong team, you must understand the importance and the benefits of following rules and moving in harmony with others. Respect that culture, and it will respect you in return.

Jan 1st, 2000
I am sorry, but it is the rule...

Part II

The Collision—Where Things Go Wrong

Chapter 8
Language Differences Are Cultural Differences

Language is the soul of a culture;
translation is its shadow.
—Author

Today, with the advancement of AI, language translation has become almost instantaneous and remarkably accurate. There is no doubt that such tools have significantly supported communication among people who speak different languages.

However, no matter how advanced translation tools become, conversations that rely on them still feel vastly different from those between people who share the same native language. The reason is simple: language is deeply rooted in the culture from which it was born.

In Japan, even in highly technical fields such as engineering, onomatopoeic and mimetic expressions like *gata-gata* and *koto-koto* are commonly used in meetings and reports. Adverbs and adverbial phrases such as *nani ga nan demo* ("no matter what") or *gutto* ("firmly," "with determination") are also frequently employed. Although these sound-based expressions might cause differences in interpretation depending on the listener, they are often used to convey nuances more precisely among Japanese engineers.

To communicate effectively through these onomatopoeic and mimetic expressions, one must share a common understanding of the situations being described. In other words, one must share the same cultural and environmental background.

According to AI translation tools, the Japanese onomatopoeia *koto-koto* is translated as "thumping." Yet, when we look up *thumping* in an English dictionary, we find it described as "pounding or throbbing in a heavy, continuous way." Meanwhile, a Japanese dictionary explains *koto-koto* as "a word that describes the sound made when light objects touch each other." Clearly, *koto-koto* and "thumping" do not evoke the same sound or feeling.

When do "rattling" or "thumping" occur? What emotions are implied by words like "whatever" or "gut"? Even the most sophisticated AI translation cannot capture these distinctions correctly, because each of these words carries nuances shaped by its own cultural and environmental context.

Language is, of course, a vital tool for communication, but it is only one part of a much larger cultural system. It alone cannot always achieve true understanding. Onomatopoeia, metaphors, and idiomatic expressions exist precisely because they allow people who share the same cultural background to express subtle shades of meaning that cannot be fully articulated by words alone. In that sense, they are not simply "language"; they are among the important tools for human communication that resemble language yet go beyond it.

One domain where language alone often fails is the expression of love. This is why poetry is so rich in metaphor. A truth we all know well. One of my favorite poems was written about 900 years ago by Emperor Sutoku, Japan's seventy-fifth emperor:

"Se wo hayami / Iwa ni sekaruru / Takigawa no / Warete mo sue ni / Awan to zo omou"

Roughly translated, it means: "As the rapids, blocked by rocks, split into two streams but eventually merge again, so shall we, i.e., though separated now, meet again someday." It expresses the poet's longing and hope for a reunion with his beloved, using nature's imagery to convey an emotion deeper than words.

In English, we find a similar sentiment in the saying, "True love will find its course." Like Sutoku's poem, it speaks of love's perseverance. Yet, for me, while the Japanese poem brings tears to my eyes, the English expression does not touch my heart quite the same way. That is because I am more attuned to the cultural and emotional nuances behind the Japanese verse than those behind the English idiom.

Certain words themselves arise only within specific cultural contexts and thus cannot be translated at all.

Take, for example, the English word *privacy*. In Japanese, it is often translated as *shiseikatsu* ("private life"), but that fails to capture the true meaning, the concept of a personal domain that others must not intrude upon, a right and a feeling deeply rooted in Western thought. Japanese society, having long valued *sharing* and *harmony*, never historically developed a concept equivalent to Western *privacy*.

Similarly, the word *humor* carries different nuances in English and Japanese. What English speakers consider "humor" is often quite different from the tone or feeling implied when Japanese people use the same borrowed term.

Conversely, the Japanese word *mottainai* is often translated as "What a waste!", but that misses its spiritual depth. The original word carries Buddhist values of respect for nature and gratitude toward people, implying that wasting something is not merely inefficient, but a form of disrespect toward the life or labor behind it.

The Japanese expression *itadakimasu,* said before a meal, literally translates as "I humbly receive (this meal)." Yet this fails to convey its true cultural meaning, an acknowledgment that one is taking a life to sustain one's own, and an expression of gratitude to those who prepared the meal and to nature itself. The act of bowing one's head, raising the bowl higher than one's mouth, and saying *itadakimasu* reflects humility and reverence, a gesture of receiving nourishment from something greater than oneself.

Naturally, learning a language and being able to speak it directly is invaluable for communication. But as I have explained, there are words that cannot be perfectly translated and expressions that defy literal equivalence. Unless one understands these, genuine, high-quality communication is impossible.

High-quality communication reduces misunderstandings and deepens mutual understanding. Therefore, when working as part of a multicultural team, it is essential to study and understand the other person's culture, history, and society. That requires effort. The willingness to meet others at eye level, to grasp the differences in concepts and worldviews. Yet that effort is well worth making, for it opens the door to richer, more meaningful collaboration.

Japanese people certainly speak loudly and make noise in taverns, even when surrounded by many strangers. However, in places such as elevators or on trains, they refrain from doing so; even small talk is generally avoided and remaining quiet is preferred. Sitting directly on sidewalks or stairways is also not a common habit in Japan. Likewise, sticking chopsticks upright into a bowl of rice is associated with offerings made for the deceased, and such behavior can cause discomfort to those who witness it.

One should also be careful about casually voicing complaints, such as the office air conditioner being set too warm, or asking why there are no trash cans, or why there are no paper towels in the restroom.

I recall going to a restaurant in Ginza where an American companion began to complain: "Why isn't coffee refilled for free?" "Why won't they bring out the ketchup bottle?" Such remarks bewildered the waiter and caused unnecessary trouble. It made me very uncomfortable watching it too.

Even small gestures like these reveal how, in Japan, Westerners sometimes fail to grasp the common-sense expectations shaped by *time, place, and occasion.* As a result, even without any ill intent, Japanese people may feel that the person does not respect Japan or that they are looking down on Japanese people.

I am reminded of a scene at Los Angeles Airport, where a middle-school-aged girl standing behind me in line instructed her younger brother, "When we get to Japan, remember to stay quiet on the train."

Understanding the customs of a different cultural sphere can indeed be difficult unless someone explains them. At the very least, one should begin by carefully observing the surroundings, imitating what those around you are doing or not doing. It is also helpful to ask a Japanese friend what the appropriate behavior might be.

If Japanese people begin to feel that an American does not respect their customs, how can a relationship of trust ever be built?

「なんで？」(Why?)
「辛いです」(It's tough)
"Nun De? Tsu Lai Desu"
He is saying "Monday, try this."

Chapter 9
Misunderstood Meeting

Understanding is born where there is no need to prove who is superior.
—Author

A "meeting" can take many forms: a brainstorming session, a review of engineering data, a status check, or a process of building consensus. It is also the place where policies are set and decisions are made. Yet not every Japanese engineer speaks fluent English, and it is rare to find an American engineer who speaks Japanese. In most cases, communication proceeds through Japanese members who manage to speak some English, or through interpreters. But in either case, the finer points, the subtle nuances that are essential to truly understand one another, often fail to come across accurately.

Even more, such miscommunication is not limited to language alone. It would persist even if both sides spoke perfectly in each other's tongue, because the very ways of thinking and interpreting are shaped by different cultural foundations. Neither side realizes what has not been properly conveyed, and each walks away with a slightly different conclusion. That is what I call the *misunderstood meeting.*

Take, for instance, the kind of nuance that goes missing: an American engineer may believe, "We reached a clear and simple decision," while the Japanese side may be thinking, "We came to a tentative conclusion, but we still need to verify more before knowing whether it's truly correct." Such differences in perception occur not only in meetings aimed at making decisions but in all kinds of discussions where subtle nuances diverge.

Let us return to the scene in the rainy elevator at Narita Airport, where one person muttered, "They did not say yes or no," and another responded, "They are hiding something." You can almost hear the continuation: *"Why won't they make it clear? If they would just say yes or no, we could plan our next steps."* For an American engineer whose cultural DNA is steeped in Western history and philosophy, this reaction is entirely natural.

There are books that explain Japan as a culture where people avoid saying what they truly think. But I disagree. Japanese engineers do speak their minds when necessary. As mentioned in Chapter 1, Japan's cultural foundation values harmony (*wa*), restraining one's own opinion to build consensus. Yet that does not directly translate to an aversion to saying "yes" or "no." If a Western engineer believes, *"They have already decided yes or no, but simply don't say it aloud because that's their culture,"* that is a misunderstanding.

So why *don't* Japanese engineers say yes or no clearly? If you can believe me when I say, "When they have a definite yes or no, they will say it," then the answer is simple: they have not yet reached that stage. The American side assumes that the meeting has covered all the necessary conditions and data, and therefore a conclusion can and should be made. But for the Japanese engineers, there is still not enough information to justify a final decision.

How far did today's discussion actually cover the issue? Did we overlook anything? Is there something important we need to know before finalizing a conclusion? They think: there's no way we can make a sound judgment after only two or three meetings. In that state, how could we possibly say yes or no?

Consider an example. Suppose a team has decided to use a rare metal as a material for a component. The shape, manufacturability, processing, and cost requirements are all satisfied. There seems to be no reason to reject the proposal. The Western engineer concludes the decision has been made.

The Japanese engineers, however, are likely to ask a broader set of questions: *What other applications exist that use a similar rare metal? Have there been any issues in those cases? If demand increases in the future, how much might the cost rise? Is the supply of the metal secure? Could we use an alternative material if needed? And if so, how would that affect design, function, and profitability?*

Of course, the American side also considers these matters carefully. Yet the Japanese side tends to explore even the indirect and peripheral impacts, seeking to confirm that risks have been minimized to the fullest extent.

How many times have you heard the phrase, *"Sorry for Japanese,"* in meetings with Japanese engineers? It means, *"Please allow us to discuss in Japanese for a moment."* Likely, countless times. They wish to debate these complex topics in a language where they can express themselves fully. If you could understand the Japanese conversation directly, you might feel tempted to say, *"You don't need to go that far. Those possibilities are too remote to worry about."* But they are discussing even those possibilities because, at the heart of Japanese thinking, lies the teaching that *white and black coexist and complete one another*, and that *everything in the world is interconnected and mutually influential.*

After such deep discussions, what emerges is often not a decision but a new list of concerns to be examined. Explaining the reasoning behind that list in English, in full detail, is extremely difficult from linguistically and conceptually. Therefore, as a result, American engineers often receive only the summarized conclusion: *"There are no particular problems, but we would like to further examine this and that."* Not only is the context lost, but it can seem strange that, after so much Japanese discussion, only such a brief summary is shared.

One might even recall Edward Lorenz's 1972 "butterfly effect": *a butterfly flaps its wings in Brazil and a tornado arises in Texas.* It feels like an "engineering version" of chaos theory, where only the beginning and end are visible, and all the intricate, interrelated middle discussions are hidden within Japanese dialogue.

The Japanese style of discussion differs from the Western approach, and combined with the language barrier, it naturally leads to misunderstanding. Neither method is inherently better or worse, yet these cultural differences often mislead American engineers.

Even when we find ourselves in situations where we do not even know how to begin addressing the problem, that does not mean there is no solution. We may not often be conscious of it, but all of us possess the ability to understand one another, even with someone who doesn't speak your language.

I have lived with dogs for as long as I can remember. There was the Spitz that used to wander around our neighborhood, the German Shepherd abandoned by a nearby yakitori shop, several Labradors who came into my life afterward, and more recently, a snow-white Chihuahua. None of them could speak human language yet, somehow, we always managed to communicate. Without question, they too understood me.

Their voices when they didn't want to obey, the gestures they made when they were hungry, the soft whimpers when they sought affection out of loneliness, the way they open up and relax, all of these were part of a shared language we discovered together. Anyone who has lived with a dog, cat, or any other pet knows exactly what I mean.

What fascinates me is that despite the enormous distance separating us from our pets, which is far greater than any cultural or linguistic divide between humans, we are still able to understand each other's feelings and communicate surprisingly well. We know our pets cannot speak, and yet we talk to them; and somehow, they understand.

Many readers may already be familiar with oxytocin, the so-called "love hormone," which plays a major role in this connection. This hormone strengthens bonds of trust, empathy, and affection, not only among humans but also between humans and their pets. When we touch our pets or look into their eyes, our brains release oxytocin, producing feelings of safety and happiness in both. As social beings, humans benefit from forming bonds and building trust; it supports our very survival. During nurturing, romance, or friendship, oxytocin is released in comforting environments, creating a positive cycle that sustains emotional well-being. Interaction with pets is said to arise from this same mechanism of trust and empathy, developed through a long process of evolution.

This biological force teaches us something profound: we are capable of interpreting intentions and emotions through gestures, expressions, and movements, even without words. It shows that if we truly place ourselves in another's position, even when that "other" cannot speak, as with our pets, we can still understand what they mean. Humans possess this remarkable ability. And if we choose to use it fully, we can extend it to understanding the feelings and intentions of people from entirely different cultures, such as Japanese engineers working with their American counterparts.

Of course, I have never heard of oxytocin being released between Japanese and American engineers during a technical discussion. Frankly, I would rather not! But even without such a biological catalyst, we must remember that we humans have the innate ability to understand others if we make the effort to see from their perspective, even when words fail.

In front of the house where I grew up stood a small sushi restaurant. The chef there treated me as if I were his own son. When I finished my homework and had some free time, I would slip into a corner of his kitchen and quietly watch him work—how he filleted fish with swift, precise movements, and how he shaped sushi with his hands that seemed to know exactly what to do without thinking.

I still remember vividly how, at times, he would make sushi with a small slice of fish and a large ball of rice, while at other times, the fish would be thick and the rice almost delicate in size. I also noticed that whenever a customer asked for *omakase*, the chef's choice, the ingredients he used would differ from customer to customer.

Years later, when I was old enough to attend university, I had the chance to talk with him about it. I asked why he varied the proportions and the ingredients so much. He smiled and said, "When I sense that a customer has come simply to fill an empty stomach, I give them more rice so they can feel full. But when I feel they've come to savor the taste of fish rather than the quantity, I make the rice smaller and the topping larger." Then he added, "When someone orders *omakase*, I think about whether they might be craving something rich and fatty, or something light and refreshing. I serve what I believe will suit them best."

Curious, I asked how he could tell what each customer wanted when they said nothing at all. He answered, "You can tell by their posture, their face, their gestures. A true chef can sense what the customer desires without a single word being spoken."

In particular, since we have the potential to understand each other in this way even without physical communication tools, there is no doubt that misunderstandings can be prevented by using additional concrete communication tools to assist us.

With that mindset, one practical way to reduce misunderstanding in meetings is to *write things down and share them as you go*. Whether it's a whiteboard in a physical room or the shared notes of an online meeting app, list the key elements: the meeting's purpose and goals, discussion points, data interpretations, what has been understood, concerns, next actions, who will do what and by when. Use short, clear phrases, and where possible, rely on the universal technical language of engineers. This approach helps Japanese engineers grasp discussions more precisely, leads to clearer conclusions, and reduces miscommunication.

Of course, there is a caveat. Writing down understandings in real time is difficult for Japanese engineers who prefer to think broadly and deeply before drawing conclusions. It shortens their "*chaos process*" and may leave them feeling that the outcome is not fully satisfactory. This is why agreements in Japanese-led meetings often come with a list of conditions or pending confirmations reflecting their desire to revisit the discussion if those conditions are not met.

Consequently, any follow-up items or verification tasks are to be listed and those are often expected to be carried out perfectly.

Still, by continually striving to understand one another's perspective, and by keeping shared, written records of agreed points, we can certainly reduce the number of misunderstood meetings.

They've been speaking in Japanese the whole time...
That's okay. Let them digest our report.

Chapter 10
The Myth of Agreement

Knowing the destination without the path leads nowhere; knowing the path without the destination leads astray.
—Author

Have you ever experienced this: you thought, "*We finally reached an agreement,*" or, "*It was tough again this time, but I'm glad we managed somehow,*" only to be told at the next meeting by the Japanese side, "*That's a little different from our understanding*"?

Is the Japanese engineering team already thinking of changing what was agreed upon? If so, what was the point of having an agreement in the first place? Clearly, there's no reason for them to lie intentionally, so the more likely explanation is that there was a difference in how each side understood what had been agreed. Then what exactly did the Japanese engineers think they had agreed to?

If you've ever found yourself wondering this, you've encountered what I call "the myth of agreement."

Just as you might ask, "What did the Japanese engineers think they agreed to?", they might be asking themselves,

"What did the American engineers think they agreed to?" We all interpret things rationally within the limits of our own knowledge. Therefore, it's hardly surprising that our understanding of the same agreement can differ. If they didn't, there would be no need for contracts in this world.

Even the contracts we sign in daily life, such as loan agreements, purchase agreements, vehicle leases, or apartment rentals, run for pages and pages. That is because the more detailed the terms, the less room there is for differing interpretations. I suspect that such contracts were not always this long to begin with.

Over time, whenever disagreements arose over matters not explicitly written down, new clauses were added to cover those gaps. With every addition, the list of terms grew, eventually resulting in the lengthy documents we know today. Looking at how many clauses are included, one cannot help but be astonished at how often people in the past must have thought they had reached an agreement when, in fact, they had not. It makes you realize just how difficult true agreement between people really is.

I myself have signed such contracts before, but to read and truly understand every clause is, for me, utterly impossible. It's ironic: a document meant to ensure mutual understanding ends up being something one simply has to submit to.

If even people who share the same language and live in the same society require such detailed contracts to ensure mutual agreement, then it is not surprising that a content has caused misunderstandings in both Japan and the United States.

Although it is not an example of "agreement," one of the most well-known cases of a major "misunderstanding" in history is the episode that I mentioned at the beginning of this book, surrounding Japan's response to the proposed terms of the Potsdam Declaration at the end of World War II. According to declassified documents released by the US National Security Agency (NSA):

- In July 1945, the Allied Powers (including the United States, the United Kingdom, the Soviet Union, China, and others) issued the Potsdam Declaration demanding Japan's unconditional surrender.
- Prime Minister Kantarō Suzuki responded to journalists with the term *mokusatsu* (direct translation can be "ignorance"). However, at that time, no final decision had been reached within the Japanese government, and the expression also carried the nuance of "withholding comment pending further consideration."
- The International News Service reported this *mokusatsu* as meaning that the Japanese government regarded the declaration as "not worthy of comment."
- American authorities and other Allied leaders interpreted this response as tantamount to rejection or even contempt and subsequently decided on harsher measures, including the atomic bombings.[20]

From this case, one can clearly see how the choice of words, particularly ambiguous expressions, can have fatal consequences in international negotiations.

---

[20] U.S. National Security Agency. "Mokusatsu: One Word, Two Lessons." NSA, n.d. https://www.nsa.gov/portals/75/documents/news-features/declassified-documents/tech-journals/mokusatsu.pdf.

As another example of how tenuous "agreements" in international negotiations can be, let us look at the Paris Agreement (2015), which was indeed formally adopted yet still left critical ambiguities. The nationally determined contributions, as ultimately defined, were not legally binding, resulting in what has been described as a "hybrid legal nature." Significant differences in interpretation also remained regarding burden-sharing and "loss and damage."

From the outset, developed countries sought to avoid any explicit assignment of compensatory liability and, by the time of the 2015 negotiations, showed a strong reluctance toward using the term "liability."[21] In contrast, developing countries, small island developing states (SIDS), and least developed countries (LDCs) had consistently argued that loss and damage should be treated not merely as a matter of "support," but rather as "compensation" or "reparations" grounded in historical responsibility.[22]

Upon adoption of the agreement, the parties inserted language stating that the provision "does not involve or provide a basis for liability or compensation." This allowed developed countries to maintain a formulation that avoided codifying any obligation of reparations. As a result, a gap remained between the interpretation intended

---

[21] Vanhala, Lisa, and Cecilie Hestbaek. "Framing Climate Change Loss and Damage in UNFCCC Negotiations." *Global Environmental Politics* 16, no. 4 (November 2016): 111–29. https://doi.org/10.1162/glep_a_00379.

[22] International Institute for Sustainable Development. "Loss and Damage: The Road to Paris and Beyond." *SDG Knowledge Hub*, February 18, 2015. https://sdg.iisd.org/commentary/policy-briefs/loss-and-damage-the-road-to-paris-and-beyond/.

by developing countries, SIDS, and LDCs, and that held by developed nations.

While these examples undoubtedly contain political or even intentional elements, they nonetheless serve as concrete illustrations of the myth of agreement cases worth remembering.

Just as in the examples above, even an identical document can be interpreted differently depending on the reader. Therefore, even if you prepare minutes or a written agreement for a meeting with Japanese engineers, it is not at all surprising those each person may understand its contents differently from their own perspective.

From my experience, Americans tend to focus on the *content* of the agreement itself—what was decided. The Japanese side, however, tends to include not only the content but also the *responsibility* for achieving it as part of the agreement. In their view, to agree is to confirm the mutual obligation and responsibility to accomplish what was agreed.

When a Japanese engineer says, *"That's a little different from our understanding,"* it often carries the implicit message: "*Yes, we agreed, but that agreement was based on the assumption that the American side would fulfill its part first. Without that, please don't assume the agreement stands.*"

While Americans look at the content itself, Japanese engineers focus on the responsibility for realizing it. So, before they say "We agreed," they are likely thinking, "Please first do what you committed to. We'll discuss the agreement after that."

This *myth of agreement* arises precisely because this critical difference in perspective is overlooked when both sides believe they have agreed.

Once Japanese engineers have reached an agreement, they move immediately to confirming the measures needed to fulfill their obligations. Have you ever noticed, after a meeting ends and the Americans leave the room, that the Japanese members remain, with serious looks on their faces, and begin another discussion among themselves? The same happens in online meetings. Perhaps you've heard, "Let's keep the line open just among the Japanese for a moment." It can feel unsettling, as if *the real meeting* is only about to begin.

In most cases, what they are doing is discussing potential risks, overlooked points, or issues that need to be double-checked, as well as the possible impacts of the agreement and how to handle unforeseen situations. They are conducting a wrap-up session to ensure that what was agreed can actually be executed without failure.

As you may have already guessed, the outcome of such wrap-ups is often a list of action plans that outline the process to achieve the agreed goal, including possible situations that might arise along the way.

At this stage, the KPI (Key Performance Indicator) typically comes into play.

Americans tend to regard this primarily as an "evaluation" or "indicator" of performance toward the agreed-upon goals, whereas the Japanese use it as a plan for fulfilling the commitments that have been agreed upon, specifically, as a tool for determining each milestone and clarifying what must be done by when.

Once KPIs are set, achieving each milestone becomes the top priority. This is because the accumulation of those achievements is believed to lead directly to the final goal. Ironically, this can sometimes result in losing sight of the ultimate objective that was originally agreed upon. Yet, much like following the instructions of a car navigation system, trusting that by obeying the turn-by-turn guidance at each intersection you will eventually reach your destination, milestones are regarded as a reliable tool: If you continue to meet them one by one, you can be certain that you will arrive at the final goal as agreed.

To reiterate, when discussing follow-up items or action points during the course of an agreement, the Japanese side, which tends to focus on process, will have high expectations for their completion. If American engineers agree to do a certain job as one of the milestones, however, the commitments are not fulfilled, one might even hear, *"Since you didn't carry out what you promised, we need to revisit the agreement itself."*

Let me present an example of what can occur between Americans, who place emphasis on achieving the agreed-upon goal, and the Japanese, who place greater importance on the process leading to that achievement.

In the design of a new vehicle component, both sides agreed that the cost, fit, and performance were acceptable. The Japanese side would manufacture the new part, while the American side would handle its installation review on the vehicle.

Later, during the US installation study, a new idea emerged among Americans: a smaller version of the part that would not only reduce size but also lower cost without sacrificing performance. There was no reason not to choose it. The logic was clear: if the result is better, proceed with the smaller version. As a result, the Americans skipped the agreed-upon installation confirmation step using the Japanese-made part and proceeded with the new, smaller design. The results were excellent: functionality, fit, and cost all improved. Confident that the Japanese side would welcome the outcome, they reported it.

After all, the new design still met the agreed criteria of cost, fit, and performance.

However, the Japanese engineers pointed out that the new small proposal did *not* comply with the agreed process. Even if it yielded better results, skipping the process itself, the verification step with the originally agreed-upon part, was viewed as a breach of agreement.

Once such a situation arises, things become complicated. The Japanese engineers could see from the data that the Americans' proposal was good. But jumping ahead without fulfilling the agreed-upon steps violated the promise. According to their plan, the installation check with the agreed-upon part still needed to be completed first. Clearing those verification items was part of the agreement itself, and carrying out each side's assigned tasks was a matter of responsibility.

If new ideas keep emerging, even good ones, the design could be left in a perpetual state of indecision. This example shows how much weight the process contained within an agreement can hold.

Continuing with this example, if the American side develops a new, better idea, it is different from but superior to what was agreed with Japan. Then, even if it is reasonable and would shorten development time, it is best first to follow the agreed process with Japan and formally close that case. Only then should the new idea be proposed. By completing what was once decided and fulfilling the agreed process first, one avoids misunderstanding and strengthens trust.

While we Americans tend to see the *goal* itself as the object of agreement, Japanese engineers focus more on the *process* that leads to that goal. Recognizing this difference, it's not just a matter of *"what we agreed to,"* but of *"what the other side believes we agreed to."*

Understanding that distinction clearly is the key to avoiding being trapped in *the myth of agreement.*

Uh... yeah.
First, let's agree to agree on what we've agreed on.

Chapter 11
When Results Don't Satisfy

To argue who is right is easy;
to understand why is wisdom.
—Author

Even when conditions or unforeseen changes are involved, both sides generally make sincere efforts to reach an agreement. Yet, despite such efforts, there are often cases where consensus simply cannot be achieved. After much debate, one side may ultimately say, *"I'm sorry, but I cannot agree."* Even when both parties share the same ultimate goal, it is not uncommon for them to fail to align on the path to get there.

From the American engineer's perspective, our reasoning seems rational and our conclusion the best one possible, yet even after explaining it thoroughly, the Japanese engineers still appear unconvinced. They, in turn, provide explanations for their stance and reasons for their disagreement, but to the American side, these explanations often seem illogical or lacking in reason. Indeed, from a Western cultural standpoint, the following tendencies can be difficult to understand.

Take, for example, the Japanese obsession with quality. The endless pursuit of refinement and perfection. There is a deeply rooted tendency to aim for flawlessness, paying close attention to even the smallest details. Of course, with more time, one can create a better product, but from our perspective, this pursuit often seems to disregard the balance between time spent and adequate quality achieved. For the Japanese, however, this pursuit is a matter of pride. In the quest to master craftsmanship or to use that skill to create products of exceptional quality, the concept of time fades away. Work that approaches the ideal and demonstrates superior quality is what earns true recognition.

Consider also Japan's culture of long working hours and frequent overtime. Rather than efficiency, "effort" and "endurance" are treated as virtues. In the United States, by contrast, "performance-based achievement" and "leaving work on time" are seen as rational and indicative of capability, in general.

Seniority and hierarchical order, though gradually changing, remain deeply embedded within Japanese organizations. Young employees often find it difficult to express their opinions freely, and phrases like "What could someone with so little experience possibly know?" are still commonly heard in Japanese workplaces.

Hospitality, *omotenashi* in Japanese, is a source of great national pride in Japan, and there is virtually no such thing as "too much" of it. To rationally minded Americans, however, it may seem excessive, too costly, or simply unnecessary to go that far.

Time spent to ensure everyone's consensus is considered essential and cannot be skipped. Following standard procedures and collective decisions is more important than responding flexibly to sudden changes, and the inability to act flexibly is rarely criticized.

By now, much of the cultural and historical background behind these practices should be somewhat clearer.

In such a society where decisions cannot be judged solely by the yardsticks of logic and efficiency, continuing to argue how rational one's own view becomes, ironically, irrational. For Japanese engineers, who are not accustomed to a culture of debate, such exchanges do not encourage them to express their opinions more strongly; rather, they often become *silent*.

In Western culture, silence is typically taken to mean consent. But with Japanese people, that interpretation is not accurate. Their silence does not mean, "Your argument is so sound that I have no counterpoint and therefore agree." In cultures where debate is valued and open disagreement is seen as healthy, it seems natural to express differing opinions clearly and discuss which is more logical. However, applying this Western approach to Japanese engineers is not effective. Even if one "wins" the debate, there is no guarantee the Japanese side has truly understood or accepted the outcome and the result is often far from satisfying for both parties.

A truly satisfactory outcome is not one in which only one side feels vindicated; it is one in which both sides deepen their understanding, reach mutual conviction, and accept the result wholeheartedly.

To achieve true consensus, that is, a conclusion both parties can genuinely accept, the goal should not be to compete over which opinion is more logical, but rather to respect each other's differing perspectives and work together to find a mutually agreeable result.

It is said that Abraham Lincoln, during his career as a lawyer, did not aim to defeat his opponents in debate. Instead, he devoted himself to listening carefully, striving to understand their intentions and underlying motivations.[23] This approach often led to successful settlements and trust-building with his clients, qualities that later became hallmarks of his political leadership.

In a different era and place, the protagonist Hikaru Genji—Japan's equivalent of a Casanova—from *The Tale of Genji*, demonstrates a similar wisdom.[24] The description can be read as follows: rather than persuading or arguing forcefully, Genji's success in relationships often comes from his ability to listen attentively and understand the feelings of others. This literary portrayal has told me a brilliant depiction of how "the power of listening" serves as the lubricant of human relationships.

Steve Jobs, though known for his strong opinions, also showed moments of deep listening. When working with designer Jony Ive, he was said to have listened intently to Ive's explanations and tried to grasp the philosophy behind his words.[25] I strongly believe this willingness to listen and

---

[23] The Lehrman Institute. "Abraham Lincoln's Personality – Abraham Lincoln's Classroom." *Abrahamlincolnsclassroom.org,* 2024. https://www.abrahamlincolnsclassroom.org/abraham-lincoln-in-depth/abraham-lincolns-personality/index.html.

[24] Shikibu, Murasaki. "The Tale of Genji. Translated by Royall Tyler," February 28, 2006.

[25] Broussard, Mitchel. "Jony Ive Talks about His Design Process, Apple Secrecy, Steve Jobs, and More in New Interview." *MacRumors*, April 2, 2018. https://www.macrumors.com/2018/04/02/jony-ive-talks-about-his-design/.

understand became a foundation for the success of products such as the iMac and iPhone.

When you find yourself unsatisfied with the assertions of Japanese engineers, that is precisely the moment to shift your focus to their point of view. Ask them to explain fully why they have reached that conclusion. Through this process, you will begin to see clearly the differences in perspective, shaped by experience, context, and underlying assumptions, between the Japanese and American sides. These insights make the true gaps visible, both objectively and concretely. Once both sides can recognize these gaps, they can begin discussing how to bridge them and, in doing so, discover alternative solutions that are mutually satisfying.

Here is an example from my own experience.

During the development of a prototype vehicle, it became clear that a radiator with greater cooling capacity was needed. The American engineers proposed using the largest commercially available radiator that would physically fit into the vehicle. The Japanese engineers, however, insisted on custom-designing a radiator that matched the exact cooling requirements. As a result, neither side was satisfied.

From the American perspective, since this was only a prototype, it seemed perfectly reasonable to use an off-the-shelf radiator, one that was large enough, readily available, and could easily meet the performance requirements. The Japanese side, however, did not agree. We could not understand why they were rejecting such an obvious and practical solution, but we decided to listen further to their reasoning.

Through deeper discussion, we learned of several concerns: that an oversized radiator could reduce efficiency; that the water pump might lack the capacity to handle the additional load; that coolant flow dynamics could be affected; and that unknown side effects might occur if too much coolant were circulated. Understanding these factors allowed the American team to think more flexibly.

We then explained our own constraints to the Japanese side, namely, that since this was a prototype, time and cost were critical, and it made sense to use an existing, commercially available product rather than developing a new one.

Through discussion, we organized and balanced both perspectives, ultimately agreeing to use a readily available radiator that was closest in size to the required cooling capacity. We also took the opportunity to discuss and clarify the potential risks of this approach together.

Reaching a conclusion that satisfies both sides begins with one essential condition: clearly defining the goal from the outset. The more specific the goal, the fewer disagreements will arise. In the radiator example, if we had defined the goal not merely as "achieving the required cooling capacity," but had also included cost, lead time, pump capacity limits, and target efficiency, we might have reached the same conclusion much sooner.

That said, there will still be many situations where it is impossible to define a perfect goal from the beginning. Precisely when you are most convinced that your position is correct, resist the urge to assert it forcefully. Instead, make the effort to listen to the other side.

To arrive at a mutually satisfying outcome, it is often necessary to take a step back from being a firsthand participant and assume the perspective of a third party. Such composure and wisdom are essential. Rather than emphasizing the superiority of one side over the other, step into the role of a facilitator, then identify where and why the disconnect exists, and examine it objectively. By jointly addressing the gaps and working together to resolve them, problems can be solved more swiftly and smoothly than either side could achieve alone.

Told you. I am ready to listen to you!
No, you are not. I am the one ready!
When Results Don't Satisfy
• Respect each other.
• Listen to others.
• Understand others.
HR Policy

Chapter 12
Hidden Hierarchies and the Role of Silence

There is no shortcut to consensus;
it must be earned through the process.
—Author

Japanese society is fundamentally hierarchical. Within this structure, decisions about development, planning, and policy are made through the agreement and approval of each tier. It is not an exaggeration to say that these hierarchies exist precisely to enable decision-making and judgment. Furthermore, when speaking of "hierarchies" in Japan, it is not only the vertical relationships, upper and lower, that matter. The horizontal relationships within the same tier are equally important. To achieve consensus, one must understand this structure, follow the necessary process, and carefully remove all objections. The reason that agreement among peers is just as essential as between ranks is that Japanese culture values consensus itself.

Once consensus has been reached within an organization, its members usually remain silent and refrain from expressing dissenting views. In previous chapters, I noted that silence does not always signify agreement but in this context, it clearly does. When other departments or upper divisions seek input, a department that has reached consensus will say nothing more than to express its agreement. Achieving that state of silent assent is, in fact, the final goal of consensus.

Any decision can have far-reaching consequences across multiple domains. When tracing the causes of a problem, one finds that they are rarely singular; rather, multiple factors overlap and intertwine. For this reason, it is unrealistic to expect that a single person or department alone can make a decision and bear full responsibility for its outcome. It is far more practical for all related departments that will be affected by a decision to understand and agree to it. When issues arise, this shared understanding allows all parties to respond collectively, leading to a more robust system of organizational cooperation and continuous improvement. Securing agreement as a total consensus among all related divisions makes subsequent processes smoother and more efficient.

Even in highly technical engineering projects, consensus among related departments is necessary when determining policy or evaluating results. Decision-makers at each level must confirm not only the technical soundness of a proposal but also that agreement has been obtained from all relevant groups and departments. Without such confirmation, the process cannot advance to the next level of approval, since higher levels will also conduct the same verification.

Whether one seeks the agreement of peers or the endorsement of upper management, there is always an important process that must be followed to facilitate smooth discussions. Above all, the most important element is quality communication. Meeting face-to-face is, without question, the best way to communicate. However, when dealing with departments located far away or even across oceans, meeting in person is often impractical. In those cases, online meetings and email become essential tools.

As an aside, when I first moved to Los Angeles thirty-five years ago, communication with Japan was conducted once a day by fax. I honestly cannot remember how we managed to get anything done that way. Thirty years from now, or perhaps even just ten, we may look back and say, "Can you believe we once managed with online meetings and email?"

What I want to emphasize here is that when trying to secure agreement or consent from others, although it is a convenient tool, the email should be avoided as much as possible.

Communication without face-to-face interaction is not truly real-time, two-way communication; it is merely a series of one-way exchanges. In such communication, each party tends to focus on how to convey their own understanding and interpretation, neglecting the effort to understand the other side. As many of us have experienced, the result can easily become an endless volley of emails with no resolution.

"I clearly stated my point in the email. The other side never replied. Their silence must mean they agree."

This is a classic example of one-way communication, and perhaps you have experienced it yourself. While it is easy to blame the other party, such exchanges stray far from the true goal of achieving mutual understanding and agreement.

Therefore, when it is not possible to meet in person, an online meeting is absolutely essential, at least.

Even then, whether meeting in person or online, it often takes time to reach an agreement because opinions naturally differ. In technical matters, there is usually one correct answer, so consensus tends to form quickly once the facts are clear. The more difficult cases are those involving political viewpoints or differing perceptions of impact. These require patience, but perseverance in discussion will eventually yield a resolution. No department or manager wants to be seen as the one whose objection prevented a project from becoming a consensus. If your proposal is sound, others will eventually work with you to find common ground.

From here, let me summarize the key points regarding consensus building.

When preparing discussions aimed at securing consensus among upper management and related departments, it is essential to understand the proper order in which each department should be approached. Approaching the individual who holds final decision-making authority at the very beginning is not advisable.

☐ **Although the organization may resemble a pyramid of champagne glasses, it does not function in a way that allows an agreement to cascade naturally from the top to the bottom.**

- One must not assume that pouring champagne into the top glass will automatically fill all the glasses below.
- If champagne suddenly flows down into an unprepared lower glass, that glass will be startled and spill its contents.

☐ **The fundamental approach to *nemawashi* is to begin with the glasses at the bottom.**
- When all relevant departments within that lower layer have been filled with agreement, only then should you proceed to the next higher layer.

☐ **At each upper level, managers will typically ask, "All the related departments are aware of this matter, correct?"**
- This question serves as a confirmation that all departments in the lower layer have already reached agreement before the matter arrives at their level.

☐ **If the upper level hears about the matter prematurely, the responsible managers in the lower layers will be unable to respond properly to such confirmation from their superiors.**
- They will have no choice but to say, *"This matter has not yet reached me, so please allow us some time,"* or *"We will report back once all related departments have fully reached agreement."* In effect, they must spit out the champagne that had begun to flow and empty a glass that was already being filled.

☐ **In such situations, the manager who learns about the matter from above feels embarrassed that their own department had not yet been informed.**
- This is because it suggests to the superior that the standard process, "filling the glasses from the bottom upward," has not been properly followed within that manager's organization.

The last point can be a little difficult to understand, so here's an example from a hit TV drama:

In *Star Trek: The Next Generation*, when the Enterprise is about to explode in thirty seconds, Captain Picard asks, "Suggestions?" The bridge crew, all fully aware of the situation, offers their input. Any officer who responds "I wasn't aware of that" clearly does not belong on the bridge.

In one episode, a crew member bypasses the first officer and reports directly to Captain Picard. The first officer is understandably furious. Likewise, if an American engineer were to skip the intermediate managerial layers and go straight to the ultimate decision-maker in a Japanese organization, the middle managers would be just as indignant. If you've had such an experience before, you likely already understand why.

An additional challenge is that even within the same organizational layer, there is a proper order in which each "glass" should be filled. It is not acceptable to assume that, since they belong to the same layer, you may begin from the right or the left at will. If the sequence is mishandled, you may encounter reactions such as *"I wasn't informed of this in advance," "This is the first time I've heard of it,"* or *"Why was the neighboring department informed before we were?"*

Key points here are:

☐ **Within the same layer, being informed earlier is preferred over learning about the matter later.**

- Early access to information is viewed as a sign of respect toward that department and receiving news later than others often causes unnecessary resentment.

☐ **In principle, discussions should begin with the departments that are most directly affected by the matter.**
- These highly impacted departments need early information to prepare and form their own evaluations.

☐ **In reality, however, relationships among related organizations on the Japanese side can be complex—shaped by history, internal dynamics, and interpersonal factors.**
- For this reason, the most reliable approach is to consult with the Japanese counterpart who manages the direct interactions and ask which departments should be approached and in what order.

☐ **Even with proper consultation, one must still expect to hear comments such as, "We already heard about this from another department—were we an afterthought?"**
- This cannot be entirely avoided, as it is inevitable when you must speak with many different departments sequentially.

☐ **When such complaints arise, the appropriate response is simply to explain politely that you have been speaking with many departments and apologize for the delay.**
- A straightforward message such as, *"We have been discussing this matter with many departments, so I*

apologize for coming to you later," is usually sufficient to defuse tension.

Once a consensus has been reached with any department, it is essential to keep records. It may seem tedious, but creating detailed minutes for every meeting and having both sides sign them is highly effective. These records or agreements should be finalized before the meeting adjourns, as memories on both sides can quickly diverge afterward.

After consensus is reached, most organizations maintain silence and rarely reverse their position. However, this silence can sometimes be conveniently reinterpreted. If, in the middle of the process, someone asks, "Did your department really agree to this?" to the previously agreed department, they might shift a previously firm agreement into a weaker one based on the collective opinion around.

In such cases, there is no need to apply pressure to the department; however, it becomes necessary to review the minutes or the agreement together once again in order to maintain a strong consensus between the organizations. True consensus is not complete until every department that has remained silent will, when called upon, speak as an ally.

This is one of the most important points to remember when forming consensus across all levels of a hierarchical organization.

Yes, Japan has hierarchies, and yes, decisions can be made top-down. However, such cases are exceptional. It is far better to master the art of pouring champagne skillfully, filling every glass in the pyramid until all are harmoniously full.

How can I pour
it from the
bottom?

Chapter 13

Emotional Reactions: Anger, Shame, and Saving Face

It is easier to point out flaws;
to voice a new idea under scrutiny is
not something everyone can do.
—Author

One of the defining features of many Asian cultures is the concept of *face*. While it carries particular nuances in Japan, it is generally a more sensitive and deeply ingrained notion than in Western societies. *Face* refers to one's public image. It is reputation, social standing, and the way one is perceived by others within a group or community. To "preserve face" means to act and speak in ways that align with social expectations and norms, thereby maintaining harmony and a sense of self-worth. In Japan, where people often define themselves through their organizational affiliations, it is taken for granted that both individuals and the organizations they belong to must preserve face. This mutual recognition of individuals upholding the group's dignity and the group, in turn, protecting the individual's standing reinforces social cohesion.

Shame arises when one's behavior or words fail to meet social expectations, leading others to ridicule, reject, or scorn, or even the mere *feeling* of being judged that way. Such experiences can undermine one's sense of psychological safety within the group. To "lose face" is, in essence, to fall into shame.

Beyond individual lapses, Japan's hierarchical structure also gives rise to another dimension of shame that a superior feels toward a subordinate. Superiors are implicitly expected to be more competent and command respect from those below them. When a subordinate disobeys or challenges a superior, it may be interpreted as a reflection of the superior's inadequacy. In such moments, a superior may feel *shame* as a leader and, in an effort to restore face, resort to exerting authority, sometimes in an overbearing or even angry manner.

For American engineers working in Japan, this cultural mechanism can be perplexing. If they directly report to a Japanese manager, they may find themselves reprimanded. Not out of malice, but as part of Japan's traditional style of *shikaru* (scolding), which is intended to correct and reassert order. If they do not report directly, however, their Japanese counterpart acting as liaison might receive the reprimand instead. Many have witnessed moments in meetings when discussions reached a deadlock, and the Japanese side grew visibly irritated or raised their voice, especially when the American side pressed their arguments with logical precision. In such cases, the Japanese manager may be striving to reassert authority and preserve face within the group. A reaction uncommon and often difficult to interpret from a Western standpoint.

There is another form of social rejection that, while distinct from shame, shares similar dynamics: when one's words or actions are perceived as too novel or disruptive. Those who feel shame will typically act to restore face and avoid rejection; similarly, individuals whose ideas are deemed unconventional may rationally justify them to assert legitimacy. In the US, this is expected behavior. Yet in Japan, even logically defending one's correctness can worsen the situation, as it may be seen as challenging the group consensus.

A striking example was the controversy surrounding the so-called STAP cells, pluripotent stem cells claimed to have been established by a Japanese research team and published in the British journal *Nature* in 2014. Merely a week later, anonymous posts on social media accused the paper of fabrication, prompting an immediate investigation. The committee reported two issues: evidence of image manipulation and a striking resemblance between certain tissue images and those found in a team member's doctoral dissertation. The research team denied fabrication, explaining that the images in question came from genuine collaborative experiments and that any mistaken submissions were promptly corrected.[26]

[26] RIKEN. "Report on STAP Cell Research Paper Investigation | RIKEN." *riken.jp*, April 1, 2014. https://www.riken.jp/en/news_pubs/research_news/pr/2014/20140401_2/.

Despite these explanations, online criticism escalated into a frenzy. Major newspapers and television networks labeled the study as fraudulent. Under immense pressure, the investigation committee recommended retraction. Hounded by the media and subjected to public shaming, one brilliant scientist on the team took his own life, leaving behind a note pleading, "Please verify the existence of STAP cells." The lead researcher, accused of misconduct, was stripped of her doctorate and forced to resign, eventually withdrawing from public life altogether.[27]

When COVID-19 struck, a similar pattern unfolded. A group of volunteer programmers in Japan developed a government-endorsed smartphone app called COCOA to trace potential exposure through location data, a groundbreaking tool completed in an astonishingly short time. Yet because it was developed so rapidly, bugs inevitably appeared. Online criticism quickly snowballed, and some articles reported that "45 to 75 percent of users are dissatisfied." The public turned from appreciation to fault-finding, and the innovative app was effectively buried. Had society recognized the creators' skill and potential instead of condemning them, Japan might have been better prepared

[27] Gayle, Alberto, and Motomu Shimaoka. "Public Response to Scientific Misconduct: Assessing Changes in Public Sentiment toward the Stimulus-Triggered Acquisition of Pluripotency (STAP) Cell Case via Twitter." 2017. https://publichealth.jmir.org/2017/2/e21/PDF.

to contribute globally during future pandemics. But that opportunity is now lost.[28]

While such cases may indeed involve mistakes, what is tragic is how little attention is paid to the innovators' lifelong dedication and potential contributions. Japan, in its excessive concern for "harmony" and "avoiding shame," ends up sacrificing valuable human assets, in this case, scientists who devote their lives to saving others, or programmers who act out of public spirit.

In the case of the STAP controversy, some reports concluded, "Concerns remain that this has damaged international confidence in Japan's fundamental scientific research," explicitly framing the incident as a national embarrassment. As though Japan itself had lost face before the world rather than celebrating the pioneering nature of its research efforts.[29]

This tendency is not unique to Japan, but in both the STAP and COCOA cases, innovation was met not with admiration but with suspicion. Humanity's history is filled

[28] Shoji, Masahiro, et al. "Mobile Health Technology as a Solution to Self-Control Problems: The Behavioral Impact of COVID-19 Contact Tracing Apps in Japan." *Social Science & Medicine*, August 1, 2022. https://doi.org/10.1016/j.socscimed.2022.115142; Machida, Masaki, et al. "Survey on Usage and Concerns of a COVID-19 Contact Tracing Application in Japan." *Public Health in Practice,* November 1, 2021, 100125. https://doi.org/10.1016/j.puhip.2021.100125.

[29] Boyd, John. "Stem Cell Study." *Al Jazeera*, July 8, 2014. https://www.alJazeera.com/features/2014/7/8/how-japans-stem-cell-study-became-a-scandal; The Guardian. "Stem Cell Scientist Found Dead in Wake of Research Paper Scandal." *The Guardian*, August 5, 2014. https://www.theguardian.com/science/2014/aug/05/stem-cell-scientist-found-dead-in-wake-of-research-paper-scandal.

with similar examples: Copernicus and Galileo's heliocentrism, Mendel's genetic laws ignored for thirty-five years, Alfred Wegener's continental drift theory accepted only half a century after its proposal, and Darwin, who concealed his theory of evolution for twenty-three years after returning from the voyage of the *Beagle*, wary of its conflict with the Christian worldview.

In my view, these examples show that while revolutionary ideas are often rejected at first, they endure because of the evidence that supports them. In Japan, however, there is even a proverb— "The nail that sticks out gets hammered down"—illustrating how individual distinction is often suppressed. Once an idea is rejected, no matter how strong the proof later becomes, it is extraordinarily difficult to reverse that judgment.

A more recent incident caught my attention. In December 2024, a senior executive of a major Japanese corporation was reported to have said that "revitalizing Japan's economy requires accepting immigrants." Social media erupted with outrage—accusations of "destroying Japanese culture" and "betraying the nation," followed by calls for a boycott.[30] Later, it was revealed that the report itself might have been inaccurate. What intrigued me was the company's response: it neither issued an apology nor defended itself by clarifying the facts. Instead, it waited calmly, allowing time to cool public sentiment. Eventually, the criticism faded, the boycott ended, and the executive retained his position. The company had lost face tempo-

[30] Takita, Makiko. "Debate on Immigrants: Balancing Public Sentiment and Practical Policy." *JAPAN Forward*, January 10, 2025. https://japan-forward.com/debate-on-immigrants-balancing-public-sentiment-and-practical-policy/.

rarily but wisely chose not to fight back. In doing so, it demonstrated an astute understanding of Japanese society. One I deeply admire.

In Japan, being different is rarely celebrated. The nation's oldest political code, the *Seventeen-Article Constitution,* attributed to Prince Shōtoku, emphasizes consensus and harmony over individual brilliance. Similarly, for an American engineer proposing an idea that is logical, innovative, or revolutionary, having it accepted in Japan can be challenging. Even if the theory is sound, introducing it without carefully preparing the organizational support may ensure its rejection. Rather than insisting on logical correctness, it is better to consult with Japanese engineers on how to gain acceptance. This process takes time but skipping it risks provoking strong backlash, even from those who normally remain silent.

I'm still talking!
Where've all the others gone?
I guess it's my turn this time...

Part III

The Bridges—What Works

Chapter 14

Understanding Communication: Give and Take

Our worth is measured by what we give,
not by what we possess.
—Author

I often hear people say, "Ah, that was a miscommunication." But I sometimes wonder if it was really a miscommunication? In most cases, it seems to be not so much a misunderstanding as it is *bad communication* or *no communication at all*. Perhaps we do not clearly understand what good communication truly is.

I'm not sure if I can call myself a good communicator, but I do know that understanding communication deeply is invaluable in a society that functions through human connection.

Since coming to the United States in 1990, I have had the privilege of working daily with people whose native languages were English, Spanish, Japanese, Vietnamese, Portuguese, and many others. Through these experiences, I came to realize firsthand that the challenge of communicating with others goes far beyond the mere *language barrier*.

In laboratories and workshops where I have worked places that handle heavy machinery, precision tools, and experimental technologies, maintaining order and cleanliness is essential for safety. Once, I strongly urged my team to improve the tools and the equipment organization and then keep the workspace tidy. My true intention was to make the work environment more efficient and safer. Yet, to my surprise, I faced strong resistance.

Later, I learned that the team had misunderstood my request. They believed I was only trying to make a good impression on my supervisor, a mere show, not a genuine concern for safety. That discovery came as a deep shock. It made me realize that I had completely failed to establish a relationship of trust with them. Despite seeing each other every day, exchanging words, and even sharing jokes, true trust had not been built.

To clear up the misunderstanding, I had to temporarily halt operations and bring everyone together in a meeting room for an open discussion where we could share our intentions honestly. The fact that the team agreed to such a discussion was, in itself, something I felt profoundly grateful for. Surrounded by those members, I realized how fortunate I was, and many of them became the people close to my heart whom I will never forget.

That experience taught me that in the limited hours of each day, countless people suffer from strained communication, along with spending far too much time on exchanges that fail to achieve mutual understanding. This is not only inefficient but also emotionally draining.

Human beings possess a unique gift that no other animal does, which is the ability to communicate through language. It is a special privilege that enables us to understand one another more deeply. Yet, ironically, it is often through words that relationships deteriorate or conflicts arise, a painful distortion of communication's true purpose.

From this perspective, we can assume that animals, who do not possess the privilege of language, do not worsen their relationships with one another through communication. However, this does not mean that their communication is of higher quality, nor does it imply that they possess some special function that prevents miscommunication. With that in mind, let us consider what animals rely on to maintain their communicative capabilities.

Let us take a moment to look at how other animals communicate.

Monkeys, for instance, use a variety of vocalizations that includes but are not limited to warning, calling, and threatening, to express surprise or danger. When they sense a predator, they do not simply flee; they warn their companions. In doing so, they protect not only themselves but the entire group. Even threats too great for a single monkey to handle can be overcome when the group acts together. Because of this benefit, monkeys also share information about food sources instead of hoarding them. Their social survival depends on this evolved system of *give and take,* a mutual communication that strengthens the group's chances of survival.

Honeybees exhibit a similar sophistication. When a bee discovers a flower rich with nectar, it returns to the hive and performs a "waggle dance," moving its abdomen in a figure-eight pattern. The angle of the dance relative to the sun indicates the direction of the flower, while the length and number of loops convey its distance. One can imagine them joyfully setting out together for a feast of nectar. After all, even among bees, a shared outing is more enjoyable than going alone.

Ants, too, form long, orderly lines that seem instinctive. Yet within those lines are sentinels circling and individuals moving forward and back to maintain order. There is a clear form of communication, even if silent. These lines are essential for transporting food and ensuring the survival of the colony.

Whether facing danger or making everyday decisions, living creatures, as social beings, increase our chances of survival by assessing situations collectively and determining actions as a group. This cooperative pattern is what gives power to form a flock and strengthens organizations.

We, humans, share the same biological foundation as these animals. But we have evolved the most sophisticated communication abilities of all, a sign that precise and effective mutual understanding is essential to our species' existence. From these animal examples, it becomes clear that the essence of communication lies in *give and take*.

There are certainly examples where give and take are the basis for building a stable society.

Have you heard of the Kwakiutl, an indigenous people who once lived along the coast of British Columbia, Canada? Records from the nineteenth to early twentieth centuries describe a ceremonial practice among them known as the *potlatch.* It was not unique to the Kwakiutl; neighboring groups such as the Tsimshian, Haida, Nuu-chah-nulth,

Coast Salish, and Tlingit also practiced similar traditions for centuries.[31]

The potlatch was a ceremonial gift exchange held on important occasions, such as trade gatherings, weddings, funerals, and other major events. Gifts often included blankets and mats with meaningful colors and patterns that denoted status, as well as copper plates of high-value, carved masks or sculptures with social or religious significance, and practical goods such as dried fish, salmon, wooden boxes, and woven clothing. By the twentieth century, even cash or industrial goods, like radios or bicycles, occasionally appeared as gifts. The very word *potlatch* comes from *patshatl* in Chinook Jargon, the trade language of the Pacific Northwest, meaning "to give."[32]

The French anthropologist Marcel Israël Mauss described the potlatch as an act of "challenge," a gift that demands reciprocity. The more valuable the gift, the higher the giver's social prestige and the greater the obligation of the recipient to return something even more significant. Thus, giving was both generosity and competition, a form of *symbolic exchange* through which social structures were maintained and renewed.[33]

I don't remember which specific book it was; however, when I first read Lévi-Strauss's account—heavily influenced by Marcel Mauss that touched on this kind of content, I thought this is the ultimate form of *give and*

[31] Kuiper, Kathleen. "Kwakiutl | Northwest Coast, Indigenous Peoples, First Nations." *Encyclopedia Britannica*, July 20, 1998. https://www.britannica.com/topic/Kwakiutl.

[32] Britannica. "Potlatch | North American Indian Custom." In *Encyclopædia Britannica*, 2019. https://www.britannica.com/topic/potlatch.

[33] Mauss, Marcel. *The Gift: Forms and Functions of Exchange in Archaic Societies*, 1954.

take. In fact, it even reveals a strategy of overwhelming the other party with excessive *giving* in order to compel a *take* in return.

Even among tribes sharing similar cultures, maintaining harmony and communication required this kind of escalating cycle of giving and reciprocation. If that was true for them, how much more must *give and take* be essential when people of *different cultures* work together toward a common goal.

Put simply, communication that succeeds across cultures must be grounded in a balance of *give* and *take.* Crucially, the *give* must come first.

Visitors to Japan may have encountered the word *omotenashi,* which is often translated as "the spirit of hospitality." While the phrase describes kindness toward guests, I believe the origin of *omotenashi* lies in Japan's historical pattern of *giving with the expectation of receiving*.

In the famous Shikoku pilgrimage—a circuit of eighty-eight sacred temples on Shikoku, one of Japan's four main islands located south of Honshu and north of Kyushu—it was said that those who washed the feet of passing pilgrims would receive the same blessings as the pilgrims themselves. Over time, refusing such an offer was considered rude by pilgrims, and the practice became customary. In this way, *omotenashi* began as an act of *giving* which implicitly expected a *take* in return, an early example of ritualized reciprocity.

These customs show that *give and take* is deeply embedded in our cultural history and plays a central role in our daily lives. If we forget this balance, focusing only on what we can *take,* then the communication can easily break down, giving rise to suspicion or even hostility.

When I recall the misunderstanding described at the beginning of this chapter, between myself and the members of the internal working team, I realize that I should have first considered what I could *give* to the team members. Before stating my requests, had I begun by asking what they wanted me to do in order to help organize and tidy the workspace, I could have initiated the conversation from their perspective rather than my own. And by doing so, I might have avoided creating any misunderstanding.

Once again, it must be emphasized: without *giving*, true communication cannot exist.

When working in teams with Japanese engineers, such as setting goals, defining roles, and managing schedules, it is worth asking yourself: *What can I give?* If you have not thought this way before, try starting from there. By leading with what you can offer, you can reduce miscommunication or rather, *bad communication.* Perhaps it even makes it easier to receive what you seek in return.

Chapter 15

Understanding Communication: What People Seek

It is not the deed, but the reason
behind it that people want to know.
—Author

When we listen to others, there is always something we are seeking though we may not consciously realize it. The answer to what that is can be found clearly in myths from around the world. To explore this, let's look at some well-known examples.

- **Japanese Mythology (Kojiki and Nihon Shoki)**
  Izanagi and Izanami lower a spear from the Floating Bridge of Heaven, and the droplets that fall from its tip solidify to form the first island,*Onokoro-jima*. From there, the land and the gods are born.

- **Greek Mythology**
  In the beginning, there was *Chaos*—a formless void—from which emerged Gaia (the Earth), Tartarus (the

Underworld), and Eros (Love). The ordered world was then shaped through the struggles and rule of the gods.[34]

- **Norse Mythology**
  The world is created from the body of the giant Ymir. His flesh becomes the earth, his blood the sea, his bones the mountains, and his skull the sky. The myth depicts the eternal cycle of destruction and creation.[35]

- **Egyptian Mythology**
  From the primordial waters of *Nun* emerges the creator god Atum, who gives birth to other gods and establishes an ordered world. Each city developed its own version of this creation story.[36]

- **Mesopotamian Mythology (Enuma Elish)**
  The goddess Tiamat, the embodiment of the chaotic sea, is slain, and from her body the heavens and earth are formed. The Tigris and Euphrates Rivers flow from her eyes.[37]

- **Chinese Mythology (The Legend of Pangu)**
  The giant Pangu separates heaven and earth. After his death, his body transforms into the elements of the

---

[34] Hesiod. T*he Theogony, Works and Days, and the Shield of Heracles.* Translated by Hugh G. Evelyn-White. Digireads.com Publishing, 2008.
[35] Sturluson, Snorri. Edda. Everyman, 1987.
[36] Shaw, Garry J. *The Egyptian Myths: A Guide to the Ancient Gods and Legends.* Thames & Hudson, 2014.
[37] King, L W. *Enuma Elish: The Seven Tablets of Creation: The Babylonian and Assyrian Legends Concerning the Creation of the World and of Mankind.* Cosimo Classics, 2010.

world. His eyes become the sun and moon, his breath the wind, and his voice the thunder.[38]

- **Mayan Mythology (Popol Vuh)**
  The gods attempt to create humankind multiple times and fail repeatedly, until they finally succeed by forming humans out of corn, marking the beginning of the current world.[39]

- **Indian Mythology**
  The world originates from *Amrita*, the nectar of immortality, created when the gods churned the cosmic ocean. The demon Rahu attempts to swallow the sun and moon, causing eclipses.[40]

These are only a few examples of the world's many myths, yet all of them share a central theme: the *beginning of the world* and an explanation of *why things are the way they are today*. It is likely that every culture's mythology contains such "creation stories." Another common motif found across myths is the pattern of "seeing what must not be seen," or "doing what must not be done," which leads to the explanation of why the world has become the way it is now.

By now, the point should be clear: for human beings, *knowing the reason why* is of utmost importance. When we

---

[38] Yasuda, Anita. *Pangu Separates the Sky from the Earth: A Chinese Creation Myth*. ABDO Publishing Company, 2014.
[39] Tedlock, Dennis. *Popol Vuh: The Sacred Book of the Quiché Maya*. Simon & Schuster, 1996.
[40] Radice, William. *Myths and Legends of India*. Penguin Classics Press, 1991.

listen to someone speak, what we are truly seeking is the *background* or *reason* behind what they are saying. Without that, we cannot be fully convinced or at ease.

Therefore, when speaking with others, we must never neglect to explain the reasoning and context behind our words and actions. Doing so allows people to truly understand us and makes it easier for them to agree or sympathize with our perspective.

Conversely, as history and myth show, when people are not given explanations, they will *create myths of their own.* As discussed earlier in this book, when explanations are insufficient, people fill in the gaps with their own assumptions and imaginations. Such speculation often leads to unnecessary misunderstandings.

As one example, I would like to present the following fact.

Jared Diamond of the American scientific publishing world, in his book *Collapse: How Societies Choose to Fail or Succeed*, treated Easter Island as a typical case in which a continuously growing population exhausted the forests to build the moai statues, ultimately leading to social collapse characterized by civil war, famine, and the breakdown of customs.[41] Around the mid-2000s, when environmental issues began to be widely addressed beyond the realm of specialists, he sounded an alarm, emphasizing that environmental destruction is such a serious problem that it could drive even a single island to self-destruction.

[41] Diamond, Jared M. *Collapse: How Societies Choose to Fail or Survive.* Viking, 2005.

His sensational theory of "civilizational self-destruction" spread worldwide among those already concerned with environmental issues. At the time, I too believed this theory and felt the terrifying implications of environmental destruction.

However, recent research based on archaeology, anthropology, and genetics has produced papers showing that the Rapa Nui society of Easter Island had not collapsed prior to contact with Europeans in 1722, and that the islanders continued carving moai for far longer than previously believed.[42] Moreover, the large-scale slave raids by Peru in the 1860s are now increasingly recognized as a major factor in the collapse of Rapa Nui society.[43] Consequently, Diamond's claim that the collapse occurred around 1600 must be reconsidered, and much of the "self-destruction theory" has been overturned.

This can be seen as an example of how Jared Diamond, deeply concerned about environmental problems, devised his best possible explanation for a phenomenon whose causes were not yet fully understood and then how people around the world, eager to understand causes, readily accepted it as the answer.

---

[42] Binghamton University. "Easter Island Society Did Not Collapse prior to European Contact, New Research Shows: Rapa Nui Society Thrived, Continued to Build Moai Statues, despite Impact of European Arrival." *ScienceDaily*, February 9, 2020. https://www.sciencedaily.com/releases/2020/02/200206132329.htm; University of Oregon and University Communications. "Researchers Revise Timing of Easter Island's Societal Collapse | University of Arizona News." *Arizona.edu*, February 6, 2020. https://news.arizona.edu/news/researchers-revise-timing-easter-islands-societal-collapse.

[43] Maude, H E. *Slavers in Paradise: The Peruvian Slave Trade in Polynesia, 1862-1864.* Stanford University Press, 1981; Haas, Michael. "Slave Traders and Easter Island." EBSCO Information Services, 2023. https://www.ebsco.com/research-starters/history/slave-traders-and-easter-island.

I would also like to present an example of a situation in which we cannot easily accept something when the background is not fully explained or understood, especially in a cross-cultural environment.

There is a publication in which Paul Alan Cox, an American ethnobotanist, shares his own experiences. It is a highly engaging book that allows readers to learn about the environment, customs, and history of the people living on Samoa, an island in the Pacific located roughly midway between New Zealand and Hawaii, and I highly recommend reading it.[44]

The setting is Savai'i, a Samoan island covered in tropical rainforest that is home to rare flora and fauna. In the Falealupo village, located at the northwestern tip of the island, commercial logging and land development pressures were causing significant deforestation. About thirty years ago, the author, an ethnobotanist, entered the village and, through repeated discussions with village leaders, successfully concluded an agreement, called the Falealupo Covenant, prohibiting commercial logging by providing alternative sources of income such as revenue from educational facilities and eco-tours.

Respecting the village's traditional system, the author invested time in consultations with chiefs and customary landowners, but still, the agreement was not formalized as a legal contract. The village insisted that it remain a "customary agreement" among the chiefs and traditional

[44] Cox, Paul Alan. *Nafanua.* W H Freeman & Company, 1997.

landowners, and that it be *valid only for the lifetime of those who signed it.*

For the author, these conditions were not entirely satisfactory given the long-term nature of the critical environmental issue. Reading the book, I too thought the conditions seemed rather odd.

Ultimately, the agreement could continue if a new generation of chiefs took office and the village collectively agreed to uphold and confirm its contents, but it still did not become a "legally binding contract in perpetuity."

Long story short, the village's reasoning was that "an agreement should be limited to what the signatories are capable of implementing and taking responsibility for," as dictated by their traditional system. Indeed, when I heard this explanation, I could understand and appreciate the rationale.

I believe these examples make clear the importance of properly understanding the true background behind things.

Have you ever had an experience like this? Imagine a situation where your supervisor asks, "I can't tell you the reason, but could you please do this?". It doesn't feel good, does it? You may not feel motivated to do the task sincerely. Compare that to being asked the same favor *with* a clear explanation. The difference in how you feel is self-evident.

Thus, when explaining your own opinions or viewpoints, the most essential element, by now you can see, is to give sufficient weight to the *background*, *reasons*, and *thought process* behind what you say. Only by doing so can true understanding be achieved.

Chapter 16
Communication Strategies That Build Trust

An explanation is often just an excuse in disguise.
—Author

When Japanese people converse among themselves, they often refer to Americans collectively as *"they."* You might hear phrases like, "Let's wait to hear *their* proposal," or "*They* probably won't agree." This "they" carries an implicit sense of distinction. A feeling that *they* are different from *us*. It arises naturally from the awareness that, while Japanese people can easily understand one another through shared cultural context, communicating with those from a Western background requires deliberate effort.

However, there is another, uniquely Japanese nuance at play here: the implicit contrast between *"they"* and *"we."*

Foreign visitors to Japan often comment on how kind and helpful Japanese people are, regardless of the visitor's unfamiliarity or lack of language skills. "Japanese people are so polite and considerate, I'd love to come back again," they say. And indeed, as long as you remain a *visitor* or a *foreigner*, that is often true. But once a person actually *moves* to Japan, the situation changes dramatically.

A tourist or short-term visitor poses no impact on the local community. But a long-term resident, someone who looks different, speaks a different language, and comes from a different culture, inevitably affects the dynamics of that community. And that difference, in itself, can cause unease among Japanese people. The question becomes: *can we truly work and live together in harmony, or not?*

When I myself moved to the United States, I was astonished to find that public schools had ESL (English as a Second Language) classes for non-native speakers. To my knowledge, such systems are still uncommon in Japan today. Similarly, while both countries require proof of financial stability to rent an apartment, Japan goes further: foreign residents must have lived in the country for at least six months before they can even open a bank account. In other words, new arrivals are effectively told to live in a hotel for half a year.

A quick look at global statistics reveals the difference in openness: according to 2024 data, the United States migrants comprise 15.2 percent of the population. By contrast, Japan's proportion is 2.8 percent, approximately one-fifth of the American level. Japan's national policy has long maintained an extremely low immigration rate.[45]

[45] United Nations Department of Economic and Social Affairs. "International Migrant Stock 2024 Key Facts and Figures Advance Unedited Version." *UN DESA*, January 2025.
https://www.un.org/development/desa/pd/sites/www.un.org.development.desa.pd/files/undesa_pd_2025_intlmigstock_2024_key_facts_and_figures_advance-unedited.pdf.

As I mentioned in *Japan as Number One*, Japanese people often take a certain pride in being *distinct* from foreigners. This in itself is not a bad thing. But as a result, there remains a deeply ingrained sense of separation that might come from an unconscious belief that *"they"* and *"we"* must remain different.

If you are an American who has introduced yourself in Japan by saying in Japanese, "Hajimemashite, Watashi no Namae wa [your name] desu,"—"nice to meet you, my name is [your name]"—you have likely been met with an enthusiastic, "Wow, you speak Japanese very well!" Imagine, however, if I introduced myself in America with, "My name is Tak," and someone replied, "You speak English very well!"—that has never actually happened to me. Frankly, I would find that insulting. Anyone can say their own name in another language.

Similarly, when a foreigner eats with chopsticks in Japan and hears, "You use chopsticks very well!" That, too, whilc mcant kindly, can feel patronizing. If I were complimented for using a knife and fork, "You use a knife and fork very well!" I might take it as mockery. Of course, Japanese people are not trying to insult foreigners. Rather, this reflects how deeply they perceive certain aspects of life, such as language or etiquette, as uniquely *Japanese* and thus spccial when practiced by outsiders.

That long preface leads to the central issue: this implicit division of *we* and *they* can, unfortunately, become a serious barrier to building trust. When even ordinary actions are regarded as *special*, it follows naturally that any behavior deviating from Japanese norms risks eroding trust.

If you are merely a tourist or a guest, this may not be a problem. But if you are a business partner working alongside Japanese colleagues, losing trust means losing the ability to collaborate effectively.

There is, however, something close to a *silver bullet* for gaining trust: the Japanese language itself.

If you study Japanese until you can speak it fluently, at a level where people no longer say, "You speak Japanese very well!", then you will find that trust comes far more easily. Think of an American colleague you know who speaks Japanese perfectly. Notice how Japanese people interact with that person warmly, naturally, almost as if speaking with another Japanese colleague. Sharing the same language connects hearts; it allows genuine understanding, just as it does among the Japanese themselves.

That said, mastering Japanese is a monumental challenge and takes time. Therefore, let me offer two practical suggestions.

1. Talk about cultural differences.

Use cultural differences as a bridge for conversation. Ask questions such as:

"Why do Japanese people care so much about what others think?"

"Why are Americans so bad at reading the room?"

"Why do Japanese people hang their laundry outside?"

"Well, Americans do that too in the suburbs, don't they?"

"Why don't Japanese people chat with strangers in elevators or at supermarket checkouts?"

These conversations provide wonderful opportunities to deepen mutual understanding, spark laughter, and build trust naturally. Topics about culture and customs are easy to discuss, and everyone has something to say about them.

When I engage in networking or small talk, I often bring up Japanese food culture, which allows me to naturally connect with people. I describe my love of fresh seafood, even the delicate flavor of squid or shrimp sashimi still moving on the plate, and paint that image vividly. After a good laugh, business discussions tend to flow surprisingly smoothly.

2. Express your expectations clearly.

My second proposal is more serious, and I urge you to practice it consciously. When working with Japanese engineers, take time to explain *what you expect from them*. Not in terms of task division, but in terms of *their abilities and contributions*.

Speak specifically about the skills and experience you value and rely on. Be honest and concrete, then never fabricate praise. Since you are partners working toward a shared goal, there must be genuine expectations on your part. Articulate them clearly.

When Japanese engineers hear that you truly depend on their expertise, they will recognize that they are needed and will naturally strive to maintain mutual trust.

Conversely, one powerful way to build trust is to avoid the actions and words that destroy it. Below are examples, some obvious yet surprisingly common, of behaviors that weaken trust. If trust truly matters to you, be mindful of these.

Just as among American engineers, demonstrating a sense of *ownership* and responsibility is fundamental to earning trust. The opposite, showing detachment or lack of accountability, quickly undermines it. For instance, in a project where KPIs such as deadlines and milestones are agreed upon and the project is being carried out jointly:

1. Failing to report progress regularly and mentioning delays only after being asked.
2. Claiming, "I only followed instructions, so the failure isn't my fault."
3. Explaining that delays are another team's fault, or saying, "It couldn't be helped because it was out of my control," which almost always sounds like an excuse.

If you remember saying, "Thanksgiving and year-end holidays slowed everyone down," don't say that again. You already knew about those holidays.

Similarly, inconsistency between words and actions accelerates the loss of trust. For example, in the meeting,

1. Presenting many ideas without any concrete plan or action.
2. Saying "I can do it" but then not doing it.
3. Promising to meet a deadline and failing to do so.

Another unwelcome habit is a passive, "waiting" attitude. Not taking the initiative to seek needed information. For example, even when someone is fully aware that they are involved in a project where they must work together as a team and move forward through a process of trial and error, they nevertheless choose,

1. Explaining a failure by saying, "No one gave me the correct information."
2. Having no contingency plan, no Plan B, in case things go wrong.

If you have worked with Japanese engineers, you may have heard the word "Hō-Ren-Sō"—an abbreviation of *Hōkoku* (report), *Renraku* (inform), and *Sōdan* (consult). The fact that this phrase exists shows how much importance is placed on sharing progress updates with supervisors and related departments.

Even when things are going smoothly, proactively reporting progress, such as utilizing email or phone, is a sure way to build trust. The opposite situation, being told, "Why didn't you tell us earlier when you could have?" is often enough to damage trust irreparably.

Among Japanese colleagues, the phrase *"I can't trust that guy"* is not uncommon. It rarely refers to deliberate betrayal; usually, it stems from small disappointments, e.g., being late, failing to notify others in advance, making promises lightly and breaking them, criticizing others while ignoring one's own faults, or acting selfishly without considering others' feelings.

Of course, these are not unique to Japan; they apply equally to us Americans. However, the last point, *acting without regard for others' feelings,* is one we Westerners must pay particular attention to, as our habitual style can easily be perceived that way.

For example, long monologues may seem pushy or domineering. After about thirty seconds, a Japanese listener may begin to lose the thread. Repeating the same points should also be avoided, as it can feel disrespectful to those who already answered your question. Humor is valuable, but try not to drift too far off-topic.

Also, refrain from slang or idiomatic expressions like *"no-brainer"* or *"smoking gun."* What seems casual or harmless among Americans may strike Japanese listeners as insensitive or inconsiderate.

In short, the points raised in this chapter are not unique to Japanese people. They are certainly universal principles of professionalism. Yet when working with Japanese engineers in particular, it is worth consciously practicing these habits to maintain and strengthen mutual trust.

What would you feel if I said, "you use knife and fork very well"?
Wow! You use chopsticks very well!

Chapter 17

Decoding Meetings: Verbal and Nonverbal Cues

We fail to understand those we think we cannot understand.
—Author

Have you ever found yourself feeling like Alice who wandered into Wonderland in the middle of a meeting with Japanese colleagues? You're unsure whether what you explained was properly understood. The feedback from them is ambiguous. There are various questions; you answer them, but you don't quite grasp the intent behind those questions. When they say "yes," is it the Japanese *hai*, which may actually mean "I hear you" rather than "I agree"? Or does it mean "Yes, there is a problem"? Indeed, at times, a meeting with Japanese participants can feel as though you've fallen straight down the rabbit hole into Wonderland.

The Japanese colleague who had kindly guided you to the meeting room—your own White Rabbit—seems to have disappeared. Suddenly, the Cheshire Cat and the Caterpillar appear, whispering in your ear: "What is the purpose of this meeting? Where is the exit? What are you doing here?" You start wondering if this meeting might turn into an endless tea party. Then, unexpectedly, the Japanese executive turns into the Queen of Hearts, glaring as if to say, "Off with your heads!"

Japanese participants seem to understand what's going on, but are we Americans the only ones who have stumbled into Wonderland? Or have the Japanese also fallen in with us?

From the Japanese side, there is often unease about whether they are fully understanding the discussion, which is conducted in a language that is not their own. They may hesitate to speak up because they are not confident that what they want to say will come out correctly in English or even that their point is accurate. Even if they try, it may not come across as intended. Imagine being in their shoes, having to discuss high-stakes, error-intolerant technical matters in a second language within a professional setting. For many Japanese participants, too, the meeting may feel like a bewildering Wonderland.

It seems, then, that both sides are wandering in this maze together. In fact, I have seen many cases where small nuances are misunderstood by Japanese participants, or where the Japanese intent is misconstrued by Americans.

One common example is when someone says during a meeting, "Sorry for Japanese." As I mentioned in the previous chapter, this usually means, "Please allow us to speak only in Japanese." Then the Japanese members discuss something among themselves for a while before saying, "Thank you for waiting. Please go ahead." We are left wondering what they were talking about and how we're supposed to "go ahead" without knowing what just happened. This, too, feels very much like Wonderland.

However, that phrase, "Sorry for Japanese," is actually an important signal. It should not be taken as an act of exclusion or secrecy. It means that the Japanese participants feel they are losing their way in the discussion and need a moment to regain clarity before proceeding. One might ask why they can't simply have that conversation with us present, but we must remember that as long as the meeting is conducted in English, the Wonderland effect cannot fully disappear for Japanese.

Think of a hiking group that realizes that they are lost in the mountains. The members stop, exchange ideas, listen to their leader, and work together to determine their position and next move. The method varies, but the goal is the same: to achieve *one voice* as a group. Those who manage to unify their understanding are far less likely to become truly lost.

Likewise, when Japanese participants pause to speak in Japanese, they are confirming their understanding, sharing ideas, and aligning with their leader to form that one voice. It may evolve into a brief strategy session, but the key point is that taking time to talk enables them to unify their intentions. Whether through top-down instruction or consensus-building, this internal alignment is a major advantage when the meeting resumes.

Instead of focusing on *what* was said in Japanese, it may be more productive to focus on the *result*. When they say, "Thank you for waiting. Please go ahead," you might respond, "Before we continue, could you briefly summarize what points were confirmed or clarified during your discussion?" You don't need the entire story. Just the key outcomes. This question can actually deepen mutual understanding, turning the moment into a useful checkpoint. If both sides' understanding matches, that's reassuring. If not, you can correct it on the spot and prevent misalignment from growing later. In fact, once you see it that way, you might start *welcoming* the words "Sorry for Japanese."

Another common situation occurs when you are uncertain whether the meeting is really on track because the Japanese side's reactions become vague. If you ask directly, "Do you understand?" you'll probably get a polite but uncertain "Yes." Still, it doesn't feel convincing. This is another area where Americans can improve the dynamic.

Imagine a typical meeting scenario: at first, the Japanese participants are attentive, but as time passes, their reactions slow. The two sides' internal clocks start to fall out of sync. The Japanese clock begins ticking more slowly. It is not because of a lack of interest, but because they are performing two tasks at once: following the technical content *and* translating it mentally into Japanese.

Now then, what is the meeting style familiar to Americans like? Although it is not something they consciously think about, it is natural for participants to contribute by offering their own comments. Thus, a meeting begins with the agenda, but before long it expands into the various topics brought up by each participant, and the discussion ranges widely. Moreover, the subjects introduced by each individual often require additional explanation, such as background information, and as a result, each person's remarks can become lengthy.

I have participated in countless meetings between American and Japanese companies and once decided, out of curiosity, to measure each participant's speaking time. The results varied, of course, depending on the context, but there was a consistent pattern: people who spoke briefly tended to do so every time, while those who spoke at length always spoke long. In some cases, a single comment lasted four or five minutes. With only ten such exchanges, an entire hour could pass.

Those who have participated in major conferences have probably often seen panel sessions in which a speaker's talk goes on too long, leaving the moderator troubled, or the timekeeper holding up a sign saying "time's up" to the panel speaker.

That aside, although many topics are exchanged during such meetings, they become valuable information for those who participate. From my own experience as well, when I join American meetings, I am able to gain a great deal of information I did not previously know, and this differs greatly from Japanese meetings.

In this way, when Americans attempt to explain a large amount of information clearly, they interpret the somewhat slow reactions on the Japanese side as a need to provide even more explanation, and they end up adding further elaboration from various angles.

That only makes things worse. When Japanese participants seem quiet and are staring at their documents, it's best *not* to push forward or add new information. They are processing what has been said, verifying it against the materials, and need time to catch up.

Asking "Do you understand?" in such a moment can sound condescending. Almost as if you're saying, "Are you keeping up?" or "Am I wrong?" Instead, try suggesting, "If you'd like, please feel free to take a few minutes to confirm things in Japanese." This effectively stops the American clock and resynchronizes it with the Japanese one. Don't resent the time they spend speaking Japanese; recognize that it can actually help the meeting move forward more efficiently in the long run.

The ability to sense when the clocks are out of sync is itself a mark of a skilled meeting leader. If you continue speaking at length or introduce multiple topics at once while your Japanese counterparts are still decoding your English, it's a sign that your facilitation skills with Japanese teams could use refinement.

In American culture, confidence is shown through speaking assertively and at length. A strong presence often earns respect and agreement. But in meetings with Japanese counterparts, that same approach can backfire. You may come across as overconfident or insincere, someone whose words can't be fully trusted.

To repeat, instead of adding more and more explanations, giving the other party time to think can also help deepen their understanding.

The ability to keep one's remarks concise is essential for productive meetings. Try developing the skill to convey your point in about thirty seconds per turn. This naturally eliminates repetition and filler, forcing you to focus on the key message. For Japanese listeners, this short, concentrated delivery makes comprehension easier and helps keep both sides' clocks ticking in sync.

Finally, a meeting is not just the discussion itself. It encompasses preparation, the meeting proper, and the follow-up afterward. To keep the process under control, it's crucial to align the pace of progress with your Japanese counterparts from pre-meeting preparation to post-meeting confirmation. Allow sufficient time for them to think through the issues if needed. This may not feel like the Western, assertive way of pushing your message through, but in the end, it is precisely how your message will be truly understood.

It was the best butter!
Have some wine.
Well... what are we talking about here?
I wonder when it will end.

Chapter 18
How to Write Reports for Japanese Stakeholders

Nothing is as unreliable as the words "Absolutely," "no doubt."
—Author

Have you ever thought about why we write reports? Considering the purpose for taking the time to prepare a report, I would like to present the following three points as its objectives:

1. That it is something people will actually read.
2. That what you wish to convey in the report is communicated accurately.
3. That, as a result, the reader takes the reaction or action you intend.

In this chapter, I would like to explain how to write such a report.

First of all, there is something you must understand in order to make your report something that people will want to read. Something they will want to look through. It goes without saying, but if no one reads your report, there is no way for what you wish to convey to be communicated. I would like you to always keep this in mind.

But have the reports you've submitted so far truly been read by your Japanese counterparts? Can you be confident of that?

It's unlikely that they haven't been read at all but in many cases, the readers' eyes have probably gone straight to the data tables and graphs, and if you're lucky, they might have skimmed the results section. Long sentences, small font sizes, and other factors can contribute to your report not being read thoroughly. The most fundamental reason, I think, is that it's written in English.

With that in mind, I have organized and listed the key points for encouraging the reader's willingness to read:

1. **Select an appropriate font size.**
   By setting the font to at least twelve points, the report becomes much easier to read.
2. **Ensure legible text within graphs and tables.**
   Adjust the formatting so that the font size is at least ten points, preferably larger.
3. **Use bullet points to simplify sentences.**
   Reduce the number of characters in each sentence as much as possible, thereby limiting the amount of content in each statement. This naturally helps to narrow the focus to the key points.
4. **Utilize tables and graphs.**
   Information presented in tables or graphs is easier to understand than information explained solely in words. It also helps prevent differences in interpretation among readers. In technical reports, this is essential.

5. **Write the report in Japanese.**
   The easiest report for Japanese readers to digest is one written in Japanese. Reports written in Japanese are more likely to be fully read and understood as a coherent narrative.

Here is where **AI** (or artificial intelligence) comes in. Until recently, translating a full technical report into accurate, natural Japanese was difficult or impractical. But now, with AI-assisted translation, you can generate reports in your reader's native language with remarkable precision. Unlike older translation software, modern AI allows you to back-translate your Japanese version into English to verify that the meaning aligns with your original intent. With a few iterations, and even better, with improved prompt management skills, you can produce an almost perfect Japanese-language report. If it fits on one page and is written in Japanese, your audience will almost certainly want to read it.

However, I would also like to set forth some precautions regarding the use of AI. As mentioned above, AI is useful, and its progress is remarkable. Nevertheless, some AI systems rely on inaccurate training data in their translations. There is also the possibility that the tone may sound unnatural or that the wording may reveal that it is machine-translated. Considering this, how about studying Japanese to a level where you can recognize such errors? If that is difficult, having a native Japanese speaker proofread your work is also a good option.

Another matter that must be understood regarding the use of AI concerns confidentiality. In particular, when handling confidential information, especially technical information, one should refrain from using general AI systems. Instead, use systems that are specifically designed with robust confidentiality management.

If you truly want your report to be read, you must invest time and care into making it visually clear.

Next is how to write a report that accurately conveys what you wish to communicate. To achieve this, you must first specify clearly what you want to convey and then acquire the skill to express it within the limited space available on the page.

Taking time *before* you begin writing to focus on what you want the report to communicate is by no means a waste. At this stage, it is important to narrow down the content. When you list the key points, they should be as follows:

1. Decide what content you will focus on.
2. Limit each report to a single topic.
3. If multiple ideas come to mind, divide them into separate reports and write each one independently.

The skill of expressing your message within the limited space of a page, in short, is the ability to summarize a large amount of information.

In today's world, where many documents have been digitized, a major change from the paper-based culture is the amount of information they contain.

Since digital files are not limited by physical size, they tend to be packed with excessive amounts of information. While these large electronic archives may function well as searchable libraries, the sheer volume of data they contain far exceeds what any of us can process at once. As a result, the key points we truly need to understand often get buried.

A report is a tool for organizing large amounts of information, clarifying key points, and making proposals, and a concise document written on paper still retains great effectiveness. With that in mind, I have listed some helpful points for summarizing the abundant information you have.

Dividing what you want to convey into the following points applies to almost any report:

1. The point you have focused on and the reason for choosing it.
2. The response or improvement you are considering for that point of focus.
3. How that point will be changed or improved if the proposed action is taken.
4. The problems, potential disadvantages, or drawbacks if the issue is not addressed.
5. The specific effects or benefits of the proposed action.

Next, let us move on to how to put these points down on the page.

The basic format favored by Japanese readers, one that fulfills the three key points of report writing mentioned at the beginning, namely, “making it something people will read," "accurately conveying what you wish to communicate," and "prompting a reaction from the reader," is, as you may already know, the single-page 11×17 (A3) report.

The goal is to communicate your message clearly and gain support all within that one sheet. Condensing your content onto one page naturally forces clarity, sharpens focus, and makes the report easier to read and understand. Most importantly, it increases the likelihood that your Japanese audience will actually want to read it.

Start by dividing the A3 sheet (in landscape orientation) into six equal sections. Three on the left, three on the right. Each section serves a specific function:

- **Section 1 (top left):** Summary
- **Section 2 (middle left):** Current status or background
- **Section 3 (bottom left):** Details of the current situation, key observations, issues, and opportunities for improvement
- **Section 4 (top right):** Proposed solution or new idea
- **Section 5 (middle right):** Details of the proposal, including its benefits and rationale
- **Section 6 (bottom right):** Action plan, schedule, and resources required for implementation

This structure ensures that the storyline is clear and the reader's understanding deepens as they move through the document. It also helps you, the writer, organize your own thoughts and priorities.

See the image below:

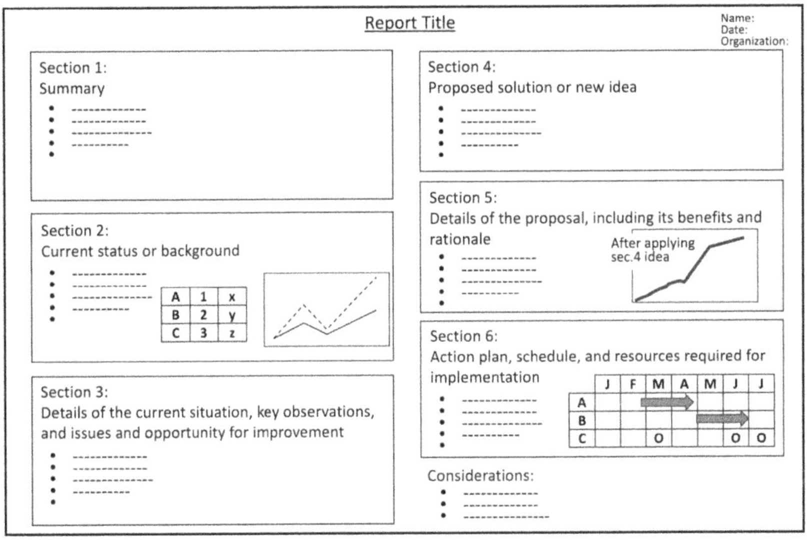

Section 1, the summary, should ideally be presented in bullet points. It should cover the subject under review, the approach taken, the results obtained, and the proposal or findings that emerge. By reading this section alone, the reader should be able to grasp the overall picture of your report.

Section 2 should outline the technical or product background—using diagrams, tables, or graphs to highlight the focus of the report.

Section 3 should narrow in on your findings, observations, and issues identified in the analysis of Section 2.

Section 4 should then present your improvement proposal—specific, actionable steps illustrated where possible with visual aids.

Section 5 must make clear the value and benefits of the proposal—why it matters and what positive outcomes it will bring. This is where you must win the reader's agreement.

Section 6 should outline the concrete steps for moving forward: schedules, key action items, milestones, and, if relevant, required budgets or personnel. In short, this section should demonstrate the proposal's feasibility.

The six-section layout works for virtually any kind of report. Every effective report needs a storyline that has a logical flow that guides the reader naturally toward the conclusion you wish them to reach. If each step in the story is coherent and well-grounded, your reader will be more inclined to agree with your conclusions. And ideally, your report should be self-explanatory. That must be understandable even without verbal presentation or additional explanation.

Let me talk about one more thing that is also important. Beneath Section 6, leave a small space for Considerations.

This is where you step back and describe how the contents of your report contribute to the broader project or organizational goals. For example, you might note what new precautions should be taken based on your findings, or how the development process has been confirmed to be on the right track. This section adds value by offering a third-party's perspective on your work.

When writing this, remember: focus not on what *you* want to say, but on what *the Japanese reader* wants to know. A professional engineer should already have a good sense, from daily communication, of what Japanese colleagues are most curious or concerned about.

Japanese readers typically want to know not only the successes (the "circles") but also the worries or uncertainties (the "triangles"). Reports should include both what worked well *and* what remains unresolved. Identifying what is known and what is still unclear is itself a major contribution. Writing only about positive results is easy; it takes real skill to articulate what hasn't yet gone right. Still, you must include such "worries" in your considerations because that is what your readers want to hear.

It is also effective to include in either the summary or the considerations a statement about next steps. What you plan to do next. This communicates that the work is not yet complete and that further validation or risk reduction will follow. It sends a reassuring message to Japanese readers: "We will continue working to reduce risks."

Providing reassurance helps give Japanese people the gentle push they need to take some form of action. Means prompting a reaction from the reader.

Now, can all this really fit on one page, and even with large text, no less? The answer is simple: reduce the content. If it doesn't fit, you're trying to say too much. Remember the truth behind the saying *"The more one has, the more one wants."* In reality, your readers live under a different constraint: *"Don't bite off more than you can chew."* Overloading them will only cause confusion and you'll end up like the hunter who "chases two hares and catches neither."

In short, moderation is key. I am no Daedalus, but any Western engineer who ignores this advice risks becoming Icarus.

To summarize once again:

- Keep it to **one page**.
- Write it in **Japanese**.
- Make it **clear, readable, and visually open**.
- The **summary** should allow readers to grasp the key message at a glance.
- Use **simple diagrams and tables**, with large, legible text.

- In the **considerations**, include unresolved issues and risks, and conclude with what will be done next.

A well-crafted one-page report, concise, readable, and thoughtfully designed, can speak far louder than volumes of unstructured data.

Ah... Yeah...
Kinda...
Did you
actually read
my report?

Chapter 19

Designing Presentations for Cross-Cultural Approval

Say not what you want to say,
but what people need to hear.
—Author

While creating an effective presentation shares many of the same key points as writing a report, it also demands an additional skill: the ability to communicate in real time. And of course, when presenting to a Japanese audience, that ability must be adapted accordingly.

As with reports, it is essential to remember that a presentation is not an opportunity to say what *you* want to say; it is a chance to talk about what *your audience* wants to hear, see, and learn. The opening and closing greetings, as well as words of appreciation to participants, are basic courtesies that go without saying.

In my own case, most of my presentation experience has been with American corporations, universities, and government agencies rather than with Japanese audiences. Through those experiences, often in panels and conferences, I have come to understand the kind of presentation style Westerners are accustomed to.

From what I have observed, American presentations place the greatest emphasis on the *spoken narrative*. Slides exist only to help the audience stay focused on the presenter's talk. They function as supplements that visually support the flow of speech. The slides may contain photographs or graphs relevant to the topic, designed primarily to sustain the audience's attention. Often, the text written on these slides cannot be fully read in the short time it is displayed, but that is perfectly fine. The goal is not to read the full content from the slides, but to follow the overall flow of the presentation. The substance is meant to be absorbed by listening to the speaker.

In fact, with skilled presenters, one often finds oneself completely absorbed in their talk without needing to glance at the slides and still coming away with a clear understanding of the content.

However, for Japanese audiences who are not as comfortable with English, following the spoken portion of an English presentation can be difficult. Therefore, instead of relying on the speech itself, it is often better for them to grasp the content primarily through the slides by their eyes, with the presenter's spoken words serving as a guide or commentary for navigation.

This makes the creation of slides that Japanese participants can easily read and understand an especially important task.

When it comes to the wording on slides, ideally, they should be written in Japanese so that the information immediately catches the eye. Even when using Japanese, however, slides should not be overloaded with text. As a rule of thumb, the slides should mainly consist of images, photos, tables, or graphs, with only short keywords or phrases to describe them. At the bottom of each slide, two or three bullet points summarizing the key point messages of the slide should be added.

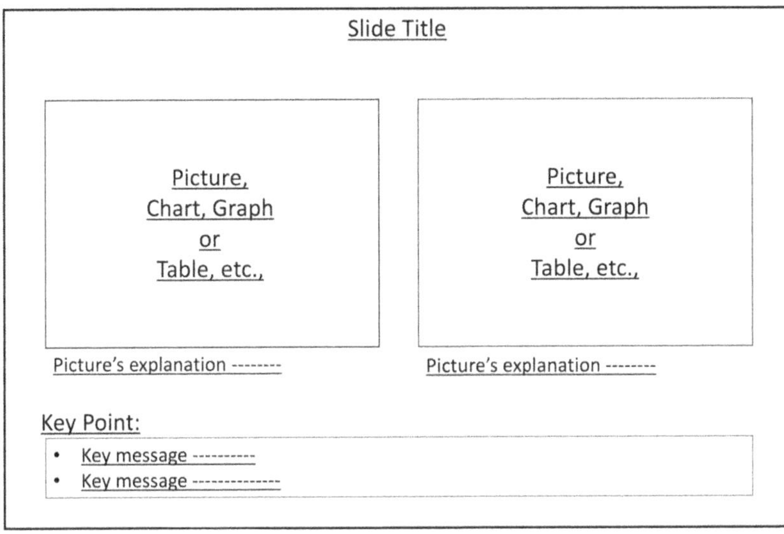

In other words, written text should be kept to the essential key points only. Such slides naturally draw the audience's attention, both as listeners and as readers.

Writing text in the space outside the key points makes the slide look busy, so it is best to avoid this as much as possible.

The final slide page serves as the "summary" of the presentation. This page may consist of text only. Here, you should list concisely, in bullet points, what you want the audience to understand through the presentation. Together with the "Considerations" section, which will be explained later, it is preferable to place everything on the same single page, as shown in the example below.

If the summary and considerations are consolidated on one page, you can display this page during the Q&A session that follows the presentation, which is highly effective.

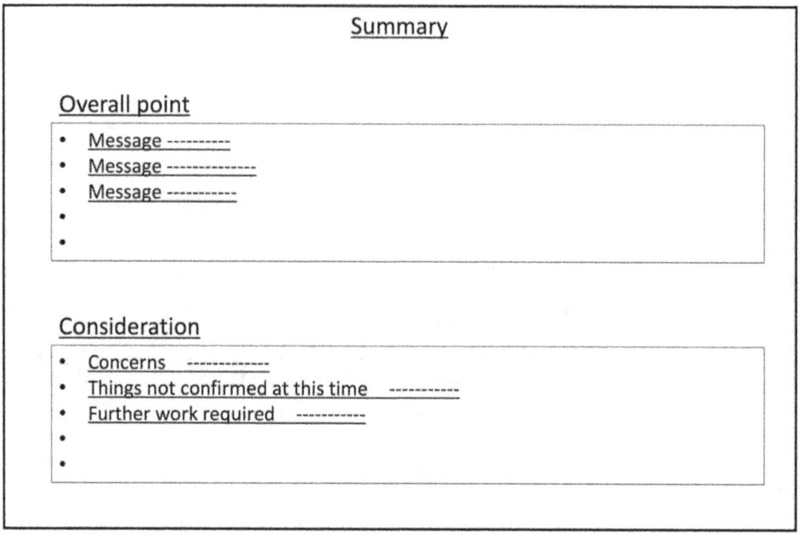

Next, regarding the presentation delivery itself, it is crucial to prepare words that your audience can easily understand. Ideally, the talk would be conducted in Japanese, but since that is often impractical, I recommend choosing simple, clear English, roughly at a high-school level, for a presentation aimed at Japanese listeners.

For each slide, give short explanations of the photos, tables, or graphs, and speak slowly when covering the key points, allowing time for the audience to read the bullet points. One important thing to be aware of is not to mistake the audience's lack of visible reaction for a lack of understanding, and then compensate by overexplaining.

While it is true that good presenters adjust their talks according to audience reactions, in this case, it is better to refrain from doing so. As anyone who has presented to Japanese audiences in English will know, it is perfectly normal to receive little visible feedback or verbal response. This does not mean the audience does not understand. On the contrary, adding more explanation would only make it harder for them to keep up with the English. If each slide's key points are written clearly, there is no cause for concern.

Long explanations tend to blur the main point. Keep your language concise and conclude each page by saying, "And that is why this point, listed in the bullet items, can be said." This provides a clean and clear closure to each section.

Follow the standard rule of one minute per slide. This helps maintain conciseness. Furthermore, it is absolutely essential to adhere strictly to the total allotted presentation time. No matter how good the content, a presentation that exceeds its time limit will quickly lose the audience's interest. Practicing in advance with a stopwatch to ensure the talk fits within the time limit is a basic form of respect toward the audience. Presentations that drag on past their limit cannot be considered professional. Unfortunately, it is not uncommon to see presenters who seem unconcerned about time limits. One must never forget that a presentation is not *your* stage; it is a space for *the audience* to listen.

With slides that are visually clear, speech that is linguistically simple, and strict adherence to time, the preparation for an effective presentation is complete. From here, let us move on to the crucial shift: presenting not what *you* want to say, but what *your audience* wants to hear.

Fundamentally, a presentation is a means of conveying your proposals or ideas to the audience within a short period of time. The challenge lies in *not* expressing them overtly as "your own." You need the skill to make your proposals and opinions gradually become what the audience themselves want to hear. When your presentation reaches its conclusion, ideally at the summary slide (which we will discuss later), what you express should align perfectly with what the audience has been thinking all along.

Think of a fair baseball umpire. One who calls a strike when it's a strike and a ball when it's a ball. Such a referee earns trust. Or imagine a photo finish in a 100-meter race. Would you choose the runner who insists, "I was first," or would you trust the one declared the winner through fair judgment? The same principle applies to presentations.

As your presentation progresses slide by slide, your audience naturally begins forming their own views. Your task is to guide them so that what they come to think aligns with your intended message. By the time you reach the final slide, what has taken shape in their minds should be exactly what you wanted to convey. If, at that moment, a listener can say, "I can see what you mean now," you have given the best kind of presentation.

Once you have led your audience to that point, you can confidently present your conclusion, that is your proposal or viewpoint, knowing it already resonates with them.

There is one more essential element to add. That is "consideration."

Even if your audience agrees with your conclusion ("It was a strike"), some may feel it was *barely* a strike, or perhaps even a ball. They may recognize the chosen winner but still feel the second-place competitor was nearly equal. To acknowledge such nuanced feelings, you should close with a statement that shows awareness of that subtle hesitation.

For example:

"From today's discussion, this conclusion can be drawn, but I cannot yet say with certainty that my proposal or view is absolutely correct. Therefore, we will continue to verify further."

Or,

"I believe this conclusion is sound, but I will continue to examine it with an open and unbiased perspective."

By never claiming to be 100 percent right, you demonstrate humility and balance. Adding remarks such as, "In pursuing this work, I may have also made mistakes," works positively. It shows honesty and humanity.

Anyone who has worked with Japanese people knows this mindset well: no matter how perfect something seems, the goal always lies a little further ahead. Remember, it is always *never quite good enough.*

As shown in the example of the summary page, I recommend adding a "Considerations" section in the form of bullet points as an extension of the summary.

This approach differs greatly from the Western style of presentation, which often emphasizes confidence. It is important to be conscious of this distinction.

Especially when seeking agreement, it is best to avoid saying, "I am confident in this. Please trust me and agree." Remember that your Japanese audience, while perhaps leaning toward agreement, often wants time to reflect further. The more strongly you push your own certainty, the more resistance you risk provoking.

Thus, instead of asking directly for a "yes," it is better to ask for "not no." For instance, you might say:

"Although today's short presentation does not cover every aspect, within what we've discussed, I don't think we have reached a conclusion of 'disagreement' or 'opposition.' Would that be fair to say?"

If the listener responds, "True, I can't say 'yes' just yet, but I also can't say 'no,'" you can follow up with:

"Then, with care, let us proceed in this direction."

And with that, you will have obtained an agreement in substance without ever forcing a "yes."

Knew it. I needed
a telescope...

Chapter 20
Building a Culturally Competent Engineering Team

Do not startle the gentle Japanese;
leave them in peace.
—Author

When multiple members come together to form a team, synergy can emerge, complementing each other's weaknesses, covering blind spots, and achieving results that no one could have attained alone. Sharing the joy of success as a group is one of the most rewarding experiences of teamwork. There is no doubt that Japanese and American engineers can work together effectively and produce excellent results. However, since each side is grounded in a culture and mindset shaped by over a thousand years of distinct history, blending seamlessly into one unified team is not easy, nor necessarily practical.

Furthermore, as discussed so far, one characteristic of a culture that values "maintaining harmony within the group" is that, within Japanese social structures, not disturbing the harmony of an already established group is highly esteemed. For this reason, when someone from outside enters and it is unclear how that person will behave, the unpredictability can unconsciously give rise to a sense of caution.

There are many explanations on how foreigners can blend with Japanese society; however, I think when Americans try too hard to "fit in" with a Japanese group, it can actually disrupt the team's balance. Thus, I suggest that Westerners remain as foreigners rather than attempting to blend completely.

Japanese people feel more comfortable and secure with Westerners who stay distinctly "foreign" than with those who appear to have lost that distinction. Just as only Japanese people can naturally use chopsticks or greet others in Japanese, maintaining these cultural boundaries preserves the sense of identity and comfort on both sides.

Consider, for instance, the image of a Western person at a Japanese hot spring completely naked, with only a small towel placed on their head, exclaiming "Ahh, this feels great!" like a local. Are they truly being accepted by the Japanese bathers around them? And conversely, surrounded by naked Japanese strangers, is the Westerner truly at ease?

A Western colleague, drunk at karaoke, with his necktie wrapped around his head, may look like he's "part of the group," but is he really? It's worth asking yourself if, in such moments, you truly felt that you had become Japanese.

According to the 2022 survey of foreign and Japanese residents regarding participation in neighborhood associations in Kōtō Ward, Tokyo, the data show a significant difference in membership rates: while 62 percent of residents with Japanese nationality belong to a neighborhood or community association, only 19.1 percent of residents with foreign nationality do so.[46] Among the more than 80 percent of foreign residents who do not participate in local community activities, the main reasons cited include not knowing how to participate, having little information about the activities, and not being invited to join. When I look at this, it makes me feel that people from outside are not being actively encouraged to participate. It seems that this may be preserving a comfortable and secure zone for those already within the community.

To build a good team with Japanese colleagues, it is best to maintain a relationship where you might hear, "You speak English very well," or "You use chopsticks very well." This dynamic reassures Japanese members that you are the kind of foreigner they can feel comfortable around. Someone who respects their cultural boundaries rather than invading their space. In turn, so long as you do not disrupt Japanese customs, you won't be forced into following Japanese rules unnaturally. In short, it's healthier to remain distinct while mutually recognizing and respecting each other's "playing fields." Such respectful coexistence between "different" individuals is what enables a truly harmonious and productive team.

While Japan has advanced globalization on a national scale, at the community level, people still find comfort in a quiet kind of nationalism. Maintaining this balance is not necessarily a bad thing.

I believe, at the core, showing respect begins with understanding the other culture and being careful not to disturb it.

---

[46] "江東区外国籍区民及び日本国籍区民," 2022.

At the end of World War II, at the request of the US Office of War Information (OWI), Ruth Benedict conducted an analysis of "Japanese culture" based on literature, films, and interviews with Japanese Americans. The results of her research were compiled in her 1946 work, *The Chrysanthemum and the Sword*.[47]

In Chapter 1, "Assignment: Japan," she writes: "The tough-minded are content that differences should exist. They respect differences. Their goal is a world made safe for differences, where the United States may be American to the hilt without threatening the peace of the world, and France may be France, and Japan may be Japan on the same conditions."

In other words, she was proposing that the United States and Japan should coexist within a peaceful world while each preserving its own culture as it is.

I understand her message as implicitly telling American society that "things will go well if Japanese culture is respected." What I would like to add to that is the following point: respecting Japanese culture also means not barging into that society with metaphorical shoes on. This is what I mean when I use the expression "continuing to remain a foreigner."

With that in mind, let me cite what I have understood from Ruth Benedict's *The Chrysanthemum and the Sword* regarding the characteristics of Japanese culture that we should understand, respect, and avoid disrupting.

It is remarkable that Benedict, having never once set foot in Japan, wrote such an influential book based purely

[47] Benedict, Ruth, and Ian Buruma. *The Chrysanthemum and the Sword: Patterns of Japanese Culture*. Houghton Mifflin Press, 1946.

on research nearly eighty years ago. Yet her observations still capture much of the essence of Japanese culture today.

In her analysis, she distinguishes between a "shame culture" and a "guilt culture." She argues that Japanese people tend to judge their own behavior based on *shame,* the perceptions and evaluations of others, while Westerners rely more on *guilt*, or their own internal sense of conscience. This inner conscience, I believe, is shaped by one's upbringing and education, both of which are deeply influenced by religious ethics. In that sense, "shame" could be considered Japan's own unique form of moral or spiritual code.

In her chapter on hierarchy and role, Benedict describes how fulfilling one's social role is regarded as a virtue in Japan. Within a hierarchical society, each person, whether a superior or a subordinate, is expected to perform according to their position's responsibilities. In collaborative work, this means understanding and fulfilling one's assigned role. However, this differs slightly from the Western notion of simply being responsible for one's own tasks. In my view, Japanese teamwork involves everyone understanding not only their own responsibilities but also those of others, like fitting together the pieces of a jigsaw puzzle. In practice, it can even feel as if team members are mutually monitoring each other's work to ensure alignment.

In her discussion of collectivism, Benedict points out that Japanese people prioritize group harmony over individual expression, which is a concept that later became central to the "collectivist" view of Japanese society. She argues that such cultural patterns shape the behavioral framework of Japanese people, grounding their actions in shared cultural assumptions. I find little to disagree with in this assessment.

Benedict also addressed the uniquely Japanese concepts of *giri* (duty) and *on* (obligation or gratitude). That is the relationships that bind individuals through moral obligation and emotional indebtedness.

These values, she wrote, form the moral backbone of Japanese society.

I would add a personal observation here. Benedict describes *giri* and *on* as social obligations and feelings of gratitude that *motivate action*. The emphasis, however, is on the *actor's* sense of duty, not on society's expectation of repayment. That is why she used the word *feeling*. In other words, society does not necessarily expect the person to repay; rather, the sense of obligation arises from within the individual.

A good example is Japan's custom of *ochūgen* and *oseibo*—seasonal gift-giving to express gratitude to those who have been helpful throughout the year.

Japanese proverbs and idioms about repaying kindness also reveal this inward focus:

- *Ippan senkin*: "A meal repaid a thousandfold"—never forget even the smallest kindness.
- *Ashi o mukete nerarenai*: "I can't sleep with my feet pointed toward that person"—a constant awareness of indebtedness.
- *Hōon shatoku*: "To repay and give thanks for received virtue or kindness."

In each, the emphasis lies on the giver's internal sense of gratitude rather than on external expectation.

This stands in subtle contrast to what I often sense in the US, where gratitude and repayment can carry more of an *expectational* tone. Expressions like "return the favor" or "one good turn deserves another" seem, at least to my non-native ears, to include not just the actor's motivation but also the expectation of reciprocity from the receiver's side.

Respecting cultural differences means being attuned to such delicate nuances. Something easier said than done in everyday professional life.

For instance, misunderstandings frequently arise between Japanese and American engineers when collaborating as a team.

Continuing with the jigsaw puzzle analogy: each piece must fit perfectly with its neighbors, leaving no gaps. Both Americans and Japanese take strong responsibility for their own assigned sections. The difference lies beyond that.

Japanese engineers tend to be concerned with the entire picture, not just their own piece. Even while fully responsible for their own tasks, they remain attentive to the team's overall alignment, therefore sometimes offering unsolicited comments on others' work, not out of interference but from a desire for collective perfection. This, again, reflects the collectivist mindset.

In contrast, American engineers concentrate on their own assignments, focusing on completing what they've been entrusted with. They rarely comment on others' domains, and then find it uncomfortable when others intrude into theirs. It's a more individualistic, efficiency-driven approach: if everyone fulfills their own responsibility, the whole project will naturally succeed.

Thus, when a Japanese engineer comments on an American colleague's portion, the American may feel, *"That's not your business,"* while the Japanese may be puzzled as to why such input is unwelcome.

In such a situation, the actions and statements of the American side are regarded as those of an "outsider," the foreigner. They are treated as the ideas of "they," which increases the possibility of being given special consideration, yet at the same time, being treated as "their" ideas also carries the risk of being ignored, opposed, or dismissed. In other words, "different" may be equated with "undesirable."

However, such moments present excellent opportunities for cultural understanding. It helps for the American side to explain why boundaries matter, and for the Japanese side to explain why cross-checking and awareness of others' work have value in their culture.

Although one has not blended in to the point of sharing the same culture, it is essential to consciously build and maintain a relationship in which both groups respect each other, listen carefully to one another, and try to understand one another. By establishing such a positive relationship, the ideas of "they," which differ from those of the Japanese, may come to be regarded as something worth listening to. Maintaining a mutually respectful relationship and continuing to remain an "outsider" can lead to becoming a good team, which is, in fact, a very natural conclusion.

As discussed throughout this book, whether Japanese people feel respected or not often depends on subtle nuances of behavior, speech, and attitude. But even with deep understanding, complete comprehension isn't always possible, and that's fine. What matters is the willingness to discuss, to explain, and to reach mutual understanding.

That is what it means to form a team across linguistic and cultural lines: to acknowledge difference, accept it, and work with mutual respect. When that happens, success naturally follows.

Even if you become fluent in Japanese, resist the temptation to "become one of them." Instead, aim to be seen as *that foreigner who happens to speak Japanese well.* It's not an insult. It's a sign that you have found the right balance.

Hahaha!
You're still a *foreigner*.
Just... a bit weird!
Hahaha!
I'm not a *foreigner*
anymore.

Part IV

The Future—Leading with Harmony

Chapter 21

The Long Arc of Engineering: How Daily Effort Shapes the Future

Make the thinking box bigger
rather than trying to think outside the box.
—Author

Every kind of work, in some way or another, serves people. Some do so directly, others indirectly. And by "people," I mean all who live on this planet. Even without invoking Taoist philosophy, human beings on Earth are far more closely connected than we tend to realize. How many times have we discovered that someone we've just met once shared a time or place with us without us knowing it, or that a friend's friend turns out to be a mutual acquaintance? We often find ourselves saying, "What a small world!" I doubt anyone can honestly say they've never had such an experience.

There is even a well-known hypothesis, "Six Degrees of Separation," which claims that any two individuals in the world are connected through an average of six acquaintances.[48] Facebook's own research has found that, on average, people are connected to anyone else in the world through just 3.57 intermediaries.[49] Evidently, with the advent of the internet and social media, I could say that the "distance" between people worldwide has now shrunk to only three or four degrees of connection.

Why do I begin with this? Because I want engineers to feel, deep in their bones, that they are magicians. Creators of new technologies that truly have the power to change the world. Whatever you or your team accomplish will, before long, ripple across the globe. Such is the impact of an engineer's work.

Yet, the creation of new technology is never achieved overnight. Think about the most advanced technologies we have today. Not one of them was built in a sudden flash of inspiration by a single engineer. Rather, they are the result of years, often decades of unseen, steady, day-by-day effort, much like cicadas that spend more than ten years underground before finally emerging into the summer light. Every breakthrough stands upon the countless, patient steps of engineers who never stopped working.

Engineering progress has no shortcut other than daily accumulation. It advances slowly but surely. Sometimes taking great leaps forward, sometimes falling back to square one after failure. People often say "Think outside the box," but true leaps of that kind are an illusion. Engineers,

---

48 Roos, Dave. "What Does the Term 'Six Degrees of Separation' Mean?" *HowStuffWorks*, January 1, 1970. https://science.howstuffworks.com/math-concepts/six-degrees-separation.htm.

49 Chew, Jonathan. "It's Actually 3.5 Degrees of Separation, Says Facebook." *Fortune*, February 5, 2016. https://fortune.com/2016/02/05/facebook-separation-degrees/.

like AI, learn from what has already been built, and from there, imagine what the next layer should be. In that sense, I prefer to say not "Think outside the box," but "Make the thinking box bigger."

In our world, ten- or twenty-year development cycles are nothing unusual. Perhaps in the future, with the help of AI, such timelines may shorten. But even then, engineering will never be a short-term pursuit. Automobiles today exist because an engineer created the first steam-powered vehicle around 250 years ago. When Michael Faraday discovered the principle of the electric motor in 1821, it was not until the 1870s, after the First Industrial Revolution, that electric power generation advanced enough for motors to become practical.[50] Only by the early twentieth century did they begin to be used widely in factories and industry. The process took nearly a hundred years.

In 1888, German physicist Heinrich Hertz experimentally confirmed James Clerk Maxwell's theory, proving the existence of electromagnetic waves.[51] In 1895, Italian inventor Guglielmo Marconi developed the first wireless telegraph, transmitting signals without cables.[52] Thanks to them, we now enjoy the convenience of Bluetooth and

---

[50] Robinson, Frank Neville H., Edwin Kashy, and Sharon Bertsch McGrayne. "Electromagnetism - Faraday's Discovery of Electric Induction." In *Encyclopedia Britannica*, July 15, 2024. https://www.britannica.com/science/electromagnetism/Faradays-discovery-of-electric-induction.

[51] The Editors of Encyclopedia Britannica. "Heinrich Hertz | German Physicist." In *Encyclopædia Britannica*, February 28, 2019. https://www.britannica.com/biography/Heinrich-Hertz.

[52] Smith-Rose, Reginald Leslie. "Guglielmo Marconi | Italian Physicist." In *Encyclopædia Britannica,* April 21, 2019. https://www.britannica.com/biography/Guglielmo-Marconi.

Wi-Fi. Even the liquid crystal display, first proposed in the 1920s, took decades to become practical.[53]

So please, don't say, "I'm not one of those great inventors." None of them began that way. Every great innovation started as a small step in a day's work, built upon what was already known. And the decades of effort that followed, spanning generations of engineers, transformed those steps into what we now call "breakthroughs."

Every engineer's daily work, no matter how routine it may seem, carries a value that words cannot easily capture. It is a value that should fill us with pride. I firmly believe that the work we do today will be admired by people in the distant future. I can almost picture future generations of AI explaining, "It was thanks to the engineers of many generations ago, through their tireless efforts, that our present world exists." The thought brings a quiet smile. That is the value and the joy of being an engineer. If we were to give up, a more advanced future would never come. If the engineers of the past had abandoned their efforts, we would still be living in an earlier age.

Still, it is never easy to keep working when the end is nowhere in sight. A long tunnel without visible light can breed anxiety. Not every hour spent leads to success; in fact, failure is far more common. When failure continues, depression follows. Every engineer has faced this reality.

[53] Blaze Display Technology. "The History of LCD (1880-1960)." *Blazedisplay.com*, 2018. https://www.blazedisplay.com/en/news/news/1749.html.

To overcome it, each must find their own way; there is no single answer.

Einstein is said to have said, "If you fear failure, do nothing." This encouraged us, in its paradoxical way, not to be paralyzed by criticism or fear. I cannot claim to leave behind words as powerful as Einstein's, but when I'm in trouble, whether for myself or others, I like to remind myself: "The answer is out there somewhere." Saying it aloud somehow makes it feel true, and that thought alone can lift one's spirit.

To keep the engineer's mind working at its best, it helps to feel happy. This is not unique to engineers but when one feels happiness each day, even difficult challenges can be faced with excitement rather than dread. When a control system refuses to behave as expected, a happy engineer can think, "Today, I'll finally find that bug!" and face the problem with optimism.

Of course, nothing makes me happier than thinking of my wife, who always puts me first. In addition, there is also a unique happiness in being an engineer who helps shape the future. It comes from recognizing the value of one's work. The realization that we are striving to influence the world for generations to come. That sense of purpose fuels both self-fulfillment and joy, and that joy, in turn, gives us strength for the work ahead. Let's keep that positive cycle spinning.

The challenges that arise when working with Japanese engineers should be seen as valuable opportunities to learn new ways of collaboration. I hope this book serves as a guide for that. Whatever project you're currently engaged in, remember: it is not just a task for today. It is a step toward shaping the future. Hold that vision with pride.

Chapter 22

The Role of the "Avengers": Advocacy for Cultural Understanding

Diversity's true value lies in
learning from what is different.
—Author

Up to this point, we have mainly discussed Japanese culture in order to better understand how to work effectively with Japanese engineers. But having covered quite a lot, let us take a brief pause, and then turn our attention to ourselves, the role of American engineers who come from a Western cultural background.

We tend to make a clear distinction between "yes" and "no." We believe that every individual is unique and respects differences among people. We think rationally, regard discussion and debate as positive, and make judgments based on our own beliefs. Instead of enduring passively, we express ourselves, believing that by doing so we contribute to society and even have the power to change it. From a Japanese cultural perspective, these traits stand out as distinctly different. As discussed earlier, trying to impose such ways of thinking on those raised in Japanese culture rarely leads to good results.

However, when people from different cultures mutually respect one another, share perspectives as they face different situations, and integrate both ways of thinking, they can achieve even better outcomes. This is the benefit of a hybrid culture. An advantage that can only be gained when people of differing cultural backgrounds form a team. The strength of diversity lies precisely here: in learning from what is different and thereby acquiring new capabilities.

In recent years, the concept of diversity has become a frequent topic in Japan. The Tokyo Olympics 2020, for instance, famously adopted "diversity" as one of its key themes.

When the subject is discussed in Japan, the focus often centers on diversity in attributes such as gender, nationality or ethnicity, and religion or belief; diversity in work styles and lifestyles; and diversity in ways of thinking and values. The associated concept of inclusion typically involves ensuring fairness, establishing psychological safety, creating environments where people of varied backgrounds can thrive, offering multilingual support, and promoting intercultural understanding.

However, most importantly, when discussing diversity, there is still another topic that must inevitably be addressed. It is the idea of "learning from those who are different from oneself." Learning from what is different is not the same as imitating others. Nor is it merely an additive process of "blending." It is the ability to create new experiences and new meaning by respecting each other's experiences and values.

In Western culture, society is fundamentally built on understanding and respecting people who are different from oneself, and as a practical application of this principle, an environment has been created in which everyone can thrive and be recognized for their contributions. As a result, Western society can be described as a collective of people, each possessing unique strengths, an Avengers-like society.

In contrast, Japanese society is not particularly adept at proactively learning from what is different and creating something new from it. This is where the power of us Westerners, who form an Avengers-like collective, becomes necessary.

We are able to teach Japanese engineers that acknowledging differences both in oneself and in others and learning from those differences leads to significant benefits.

We Americans are not merely saying, "Be different" or "Engage with us." Rather, we are sharing our experience of *learning from difference,* namely what new abilities we have gained from that process, and what benefits those abilities have brought.

You don't need superpowers to be one of the Avengers. Yet, in a sense, every one of us who grew up in a Western cultural environment *is* an Avenger. We were raised in a setting that nurtures individuality, and through our own efforts we have developed unique strengths. It would be a mistake to think, "I'm no Avenger because I don't have extraordinary powers." Each of us carries distinct experiences and abilities that make us part of that collective of "Avengers."

Some among us excel at discerning the direction of a project by gathering insights from political trends, corporate movements, and social voices. Others have spent years conducting academic or industrial research. Some are highly skilled at evaluating supplier capabilities and determining design directions that balance value and cost. Others have strong abilities in listening to diverse opinions and building consensus. You, too, can surely name several of your own distinct strengths.

How did we acquire these abilities? Most likely, by seizing opportunities to apply them, studying in unique ways, and making steady efforts through long experience.

Let us communicate to Japanese people the importance of making such efforts and the value and outcomes that result from them. By doing so, Japanese engineers will gain a deeper understanding of the true meaning of diversity and will, I believe, be able to put it into practice more effectively than they do now. However, this task is also not an easy one.

Human beings, however, have a tendency to exclude what is different. Even when we do not reject difference outright, we often merely tolerate it, without truly learning from it. What is different lies outside our familiar and comfortable *safety zone*. Simply stepping outside that zone can feel uneasy, let alone learning something from it. And yet, that unfamiliar territory is without question a treasure trove. A rich source of invaluable discoveries. To learn from the unknown is both noble and profoundly beneficial.

Despite that, people often reject truth not for rational reasons, but to protect their self-image and the order of their society. Accepting unfamiliar knowledge as true or valuable can mean admitting that one's previous understanding was mistaken. A realization many instinctively resist.

To understand this reality, I would like to look at examples from the past in which something was extremely useful, yet because it was different, it tended to provoke anxiety and suspicion, and was even rejected.

History offers many examples. When Einstein first proposed the theory of relativity, many scientists reacted with skepticism. The idea that time and space could vary depending on the observer was simply too radical to accept easily.

Similarly, in the early nineteenth century, when Louis Pasteur and Robert Koch advanced the germ theory of disease, most physicians still believed that illness came from "bad air" or divine punishment. Even after microorganisms were seen under the microscope, many refused to believe these could be the cause of disease.[54]

When Oswald Avery and his colleagues at the Rockefeller Institute demonstrated conclusively in 1944 that DNA is the genetic material, many biologists rejected it. They insisted that proteins, being more complex, must be the essence of life, while DNA, with its "simple structure," could not possibly hold such sophisticated information. It took nearly a decade before the truth of their discovery was finally accepted.[55]

I still remember when Toyota first unveiled the hybrid Prius, combining an engine with a battery-powered motor; few believed it would achieve better fuel efficiency. The

---

[54] Britannica. "Germ Theory | Medicine." In *Encyclopædia Britannica*, April 11, 2019. https://www.britannica.com/science/germ-theory.

[55] Hernandez, Victoria. "'Studies on the Chemical Nature of the Substance Inducing Transformation of Pneumococcal Types: Induction of Transformation by a Desoxyribonucleic Acid Fraction Isolated from Pneumococcus Type III' (1944) by Oswald Avery, Colin MacLeod and Maclyn McCarty." embryo.asu.edu, July 8, 2019. https://embryo.asu.edu/pages/studies-chemical-nature-substance-inducing-transformation-pneumococcal-types-induction.

system was heavier, more complex, and less mechanically efficient. By all technical reasoning, it should have performed worse. Yet it proved otherwise. This happened not in medieval times, but in our modern, data-driven age.

Even experts, perhaps *especially* experts, find it difficult to learn from what is different. Yet the ability to generate new ideas from those very differences is one of the remarkable capacities we possess.

How about examples in which new ideas were created from something different?

Consider the printing press. Gutenberg's revolutionary invention arose from combining the screw-press technology used in winemaking with movable metal type, enabling mass printing in medieval Europe.[56]

Or in the arts: when Japanese *ukiyo-e* woodblock prints reached nineteenth-century France, their bold compositions and flat planes of color inspired Monet, Van Gogh, and other Impressionists to transform Western art.[57]

Likewise, when African rhythms and improvisational traditions merged with Western harmony, jazz was born. A completely new musical form.[58]

These are but a few examples of the creative power that emerges from learning across differences.

---

[56] Augustyn, Adam. "Printing Press." In *Encyclopædia Britannica,* December 14, 2018. https://www.britannica.com/technology/printing-press.

[57] Varns, Nico. "How Japanese Ukiyo-e Influenced Western Impressionism." *Soonways.com*, 2025. https://soonways.com/articles/how-japanese-ukiyo-e-influenced-western-impressionism.

[58] PlaylistSound. "How African Rhythms Shaped Western Music over the Centuries." *PlaylistSound*, October 12, 2024. https://playlistsound.com/music/how-african-rhythms-shaped-western-music-over-the-centuries.

Sometimes, we even discover that what seemed different at first actually shares the same underlying intent or philosophy. Across East and West, past and present, finding these common human foundations can lead to products and ideas that resonate broadly with global markets.

You may have heard that Steve Jobs, deeply influenced by Zen, incorporated its minimalist philosophy into Apple's product designs after recognizing parallels between Zen and the minimalist art movement born in 1960s New York.[59]

Similarly, in *The Tao of Physics*, physicist Fritjof Capra revealed how Eastern thought, specifically Taoism, and Western quantum physics converge in their understanding of the universe.[60]

I believe that the ability to learn from what is different and to strengthen one's capabilities resembles our immune system. By being exposed to bacteria, we acquire new resistance. If we avoid risk and are never exposed to new bacteria, that ability cannot develop.

Japanese culture, by contrast, tends toward the latter: it does not outright reject what is different, but it is rarely proactive in embracing it.

There are many ways in which we, American, can help Japanese society, and one example is Japan's venture capital business.

---

[59] Karr, Felipe. "Steve Jobs' Design Philosophy: Art & Technology." *Estudio Karr*, February 13, 2025. https://estudiokarr.com/journal/steve-jobs-design-philosophy-lessons-in-simplicity-and-excellence.

[60] Capra, Fritjof. *The Tao of Physics*. Shambhala Publications, 1975.

In an International Monetary Fund paper and report, a comparison is cited between the number of unicorn startup companies valued at over US$1 billion, which are privately owned and not listed on a share market in Japan and the United States: Japan had seven in 2023, while the United States had 653 in the same year.[61] It is certainly true that factors such as "market size" (the population of startups), "capital markets" (IPOs and M&A opportunities), "ecosystem maturity" (stable funding supply, advisory networks, and talent availability), and the "depth of the exit market" have a major impact, and I understand that the United States and Japan cannot be evaluated on an equal basis. Even so, the report discusses one major difference: "investors' risk tolerance." US venture capital tends to have a strong culture of high-growth strategies and acceptance of failure, whereas Japan is comparatively risk-averse. As a result of cultural and institutional factors, characteristics such as a "conservative entrepreneurial spirit," "low risk tolerance," and an "insufficient environment for accepting failure" are described as influencing the growth of Japan's Venture Capital ecosystem.

Because I believe that startups are one of the essential foundations of a prosperous economy, I think it would be beneficial for Japanese Venture Capital to become more American in its approach. To achieve this, I believe that American experience should be passed on to Japan more extensively, so that Japan can become more accepting of different levels of risk and of business models that differ from tradition, and so that more of these ventures can succeed.

[61] Fendoglu, Salih, and TengTeng Xu. *Startups and Venture Capital in Japan.* International Monetary Fund, 2024.

This is exactly one of the good examples where they need the American Avengers to reach out and pull them forward.

When working on a project with Japanese people, in order to maximize the benefits of working in a hybrid format, it is essential for Japanese engineers to incorporate differing viewpoints and ideas and to become members of the Avengers.

Let us explain to them in concrete terms what kinds of experiences and efforts enabled each of us to acquire our individual abilities and become Avengers in our respective areas of expertise, and what kinds of benefits we have gained as a result.

By doing so, Japanese engineers will come to see us not as a single, homogeneous group of "them," but as individual Avengers, each with distinctive talents to respect and learn from. That mutual understanding will surely lead to even stronger, more creative teams.

We'll awaken your true power.
Uh... Thank you, I guess.

Chapter 23
Understanding the True Role of the Global Engineer

Think Japan is slow?
You're using the wrong approach.
—Author

What does it mean to be a "global engineer"? You might wonder why I have deliberately chosen to use the adjective *global* here. Today, we may reside within the borders of countries like the United States or Japan, but in reality, we all share life together on this small planet called Earth.

About 150 years ago, during the American frontier era, I learned it took nearly half a year to travel from the East Coast to the West Coast by horse-drawn carriage. Even under favorable conditions, crossing the Pacific Ocean took about twenty days, and such voyages carried significant risks as well as long delays. In those times, the world was vast and expansive. America, Europe, India, and Japan all felt far apart from one another. But how about today?

Since the 1990s, the word *global* has entered our everyday language. Now, within a single day, one can travel to nearly any place on Earth. More than eight billion people live close enough that, in theory, they could meet within twenty-four hours, sharing the same air, environment, and planet. We truly live together in an incredibly small and interconnected world.

In such a tightly connected society, contributing to humanity through technology development naturally means contributing to the world itself. Perhaps it is unnecessary to emphasize the word *global*. Yet, more often than not, we tend to see the world only within the limits of our immediate surroundings, failing to recognize what the larger world expects from us. In that sense, consciously reminding ourselves of the word *global* still carries meaning.

So then, what does it mean to "meet the world's expectations"? There can be many interpretations, but if I, an engineer, were asked, I would answer: it is the ability to introduce the right product to the market at the right time. The ability to offer what the market truly desires.

To cultivate such an ability, one must be capable of harmonizing product development with the creation of goods that the market will accept. A *product* is what engineers create by fully applying their technical skills and expertise. High-quality, well-crafted innovations. A *commodity*, on the other hand, is something the market actually wants. No matter how skilled the engineers or how advanced the product, if it is not accepted by the market, the outcome will inevitably be disappointing.

No one will buy a hydrogen-powered car, no matter how environmentally friendly or well-engineered it is, if there are no hydrogen fueling stations. It may be an excellent product but it is not a viable commodity. This is an extreme example, but similar mismatches can occur anywhere if one fails to broaden one's perspective and study the market carefully. Moreover, markets around the world differ vastly due to laws, environments, customs, and histories. What people desire in one country will not necessarily be the same in another.

To develop products that meet the specific needs of different markets, an engineer must understand the target market's language, customs, history, and government policies. Among these, understanding the market's *history* is particularly vital.

History is often thought of as a record of past events frozen in time, separate from the present. But that view is mistaken. History is the continuous accumulation of human experiences, from the first people who have lived in the region since time immemorial to the lives they led each day, and the choices and developments that have led to the present. Just as we are shaping the world of the future, every day of the past has shaped the world we live in today. The past, present, and future are not separate; they are all contained within this very moment. By deeply studying history, one can sharpen one's ability to identify the true needs of a market.

Of course, obtaining data from specialized market research firms can be helpful. However, most such research focuses on current conditions or future projections. Rarely do we encounter market analyses grounded in centuries of historical trends. Yet, just as our cultures are built upon the layers of our own histories, exploring the past can reveal much: how products were accepted, whether a region tends to embrace government-driven initiatives, whether it readily adopts new products, whether trends strongly influence purchasing behavior, or whether durability is valued above novelty. Such insights are invaluable for engineers.

For instance, in some Middle Eastern countries, products or games containing “magical” or “idol-worship” elements, such as Pokémon, are restricted for educational reasons.[62]

A Thai apparel brand has come under fire for using a photo of a monk on a T-shirt.[63]

In Singapore, the sale of chewing gum is prohibited to maintain public cleanliness.[64]

Conversely, consider how regional history has created markets elsewhere:

In France, a rich tradition of perfumery developed from the Baroque era under Louis XIV, making fragrance an art form.[65]

---

[62] Ockerman, Emma. “Saudi Clerics Remind Followers That Pokémon Violates Islamic Beliefs.” TIME, July 20, 2016. https://time.com/4414770/saudi-arabia-islam-pokemon-go/.

[63] Ashworth, Caitlin. “Monk’s Image on American Brand Shirt Draws Criticism from Thai Buddhists.” Thaiger, February 18, 2021. https://thethaiger.com/news/national/monks-image-on-american-brand-shirt-draws-criticism-from-thai-buddhists.

[64] The Economic Times. “10 Rules to Know before Travelling to Singapore.” *The Economic Times*, April 27, 2025. https://economictimes.indiatimes.com/nri/visit/10-rules-to-know-before-travelling-to-singapore-flights-delhi-to-changi-airport-visa-stays-hotels-food-place-to-explore/no-chewing-gum/slideshow/120661615.cms.

[65] The Perfume Society. “Louis XIV: ‘the Sweetest-Smelling King of All.’” *The Perfume Society,* n.d. https://perfumesociety.org/history/louis-xiv-the-sweetest-smelling-king-of-all/.

In Italy, during the Second Industrial Revolution, the espresso was born from urban workers' demand for a strong coffee that could be drunk quickly.[66]

In rainy Britain, Thomas Burberry's invention of the raincoat met the needs of outdoor workers to withstand the unpredictable British weather.[67]

In Geneva, after the Reformation banned the making of jewelry, goldsmiths redirected their craft into watchmaking, giving birth to the Swiss watch industry.[68]

In America, jeans were created as durable workwear for miners during the nineteenth-century Gold Rush.[69]

And in the Islamic world, where alcohol is prohibited, Arabic coffee evolved into a symbol of hospitality and social bonding.[70]

In Japan, instant ramen, now a global symbol of Asian cuisine, emerged after World War II, born out of food shortages and the need for convenient, long-lasting meals during rapid economic recovery.[71]

---

[66] Farkas, Lauren. "How Italy's Industrial Revolution Helped Create the First Espresso." *Daily Meal,* February 24, 2024. https://www.thedailymeal.com/1520233/italy-industrial-revolution-origin-espresso/.

[67] Burberry. "The History of the Trench Coat." *Burberry.com,* 2024. https://us.burberry.com/c/burberry-world/heritage/trench-coat/.

[68] Girardet, Edward. "Geneva's Watch Heritage: A Historian's Perspective." *Global Geneva,* March 13, 2025. https://www.global-geneva.com/geneva/watches/geneva-s-watch-heritage-a-historian-s-perspective.

[69] The New Internationalist Team. "The Blue Jeans Story." *New Internationalist,* June 5, 1998. https://newint.org/features/1998/06/05/blue.

[70] UNESCO. "UNESCO - Arabic Coffee, a Symbol of Generosity." *UNESCO,* 2024. https://ich.unesco.org/en/RL/arabic-coffee-a-symbol-of-generosity-02111.

[71] HISTORY.com Editors. "Momofuku Ando Creates the First Mass-Market Instant Ramen." *HISTORY,* May 10, 2024. https://www.history.com/this-day-in-history/august-25/first-instant-ramen-invented-momofuku-ando-1958.

Countless products around the world have been born from local needs and historical circumstances. This also means that by studying each region's history and context, one can accurately understand what is truly required there. What all these products share is the creativity that arises under constraints, such as the fusion of human ingenuity with local resources, climates, and values, forming cultures that evolve over time from past to future.

After studying culture and history, the next step, very challenging though, is to learn the language of the target market. Once you understand the language, new information naturally flows toward you. You can explore markets firsthand and hear directly from the people who live there, unfiltered. If you rely solely on interpreters, you risk missing the subtleties that matter most. Moreover, users themselves often do not know how they feel about a product until they hold it in their hands. There is no substitute for seeing and hearing the market with your own eyes and ears. The ability to do this, to understand the local language, is one of the most valuable skills a global engineer can possess.

Just as knowing the past helps us understand the present, knowing the present helps us anticipate the future. In looking ahead, it is important to balance *long-term* and *short-term* visions and develop products based on both.

Asking the market what it will want in the future is almost impossible. The market can react to new products; they may be accepted or rejected, but it cannot foresee its own future desires. Predicting that future is the role of engineers.

When envisioning the future, we must not think only along the axis of time; we must also consider *market scale,* that is the geography. Long-term vision requires looking beyond narrow or localized markets toward a broader scope. The longer the time horizon, the wider the arc of potential markets, like the opening of a fan. What comes into view, ultimately, is the *global market*.

Consider how smartphones have now spread to nearly every country in the world, that is the clear demonstration of this principle. Long-term planning must involve thinking about what products should be developed for the global market. In the years ahead, globally accepted innovations in environmental sustainability and AI applications will continue to lead this trend.

At the same time, in our rapidly changing society, we must possess the agility to introduce the right products at the right moments, in harmony with long-term goals. This is what I call the *short-term vision*. While developing products for the future, companies must also strategically release intermediate products that pave the way for global acceptance. These shorter-term launches must take into account infrastructure readiness, pricing, and other environmental factors to ensure successful timing.

We can see this kind of strategic timing clearly in many Silicon Valley companies. They often seem to guide market change rather than simply respond to it, introducing new products at precisely the right moment.

Apple, for instance, had been developing tablet prototypes since the early 2000s, but it waited until touchscreen technology and mobile OS maturity reached the right stage before launching the iPad in 2010, then instantly defining the tablet market.[72]

Zoom was officially released in 2013 but was initially little known outside corporate use. By refining its user interface, ensuring stable connections, and offering superior audio and video quality, Zoom positioned itself strategically. When the COVID-19 pandemic struck in 2020, it was ready, and became the global synonym for online meetings.[73]

Tesla, founded in 2003, faced years of resistance to electric vehicles. Yet it focused on creating a high-performance luxury sports EV that surpassed gasoline cars in acceleration. When the Obama administration promoted clean energy policies and EV subsidies, Tesla launched the Model S in 2012, perfectly timed to ride the wave of public interest in environmental technology.[74]

Netflix, too, foresaw the streaming era long before it arrived. While DVDs still dominated, it prepared the groundwork such as broadband internet, licensing agreements, and changing viewer habits. Then launched its streaming service in 2007, eventually becoming one of the world's largest video platforms and a producer of award-winning original content.[75]

---

[72] AppleInsider Staff. "Court Filing Reveals Apple's iPad Prototype from Early 2000s." *AppleInsider*, July 18, 2012. https://appleinsider.com/articles/12/07/18/court_filing_reveals_apples_ipad_prototype_from_early_2000s.

[73] Curry, David. "Zoom Revenue and Usage Statistics (2020)." *Business of Apps*, January 8, 2024. https://www.businessofapps.com/data/zoom-statistics/.

[74] Auburn University Center for Ethical Organizational Cultures. "Chapter 3: TESLA Accelerates the Transition to Sustainable Energy." *Cliffsnotes*, 2024. https://www.cliffsnotes.com/study-notes/20027479.

[75] Mahtani, Sunil. "Netflix, Inc." *EBSCO Information Services*, 2024. https://www.ebsco.com/research-starters/computer-science/netflix-inc.

Let me share one more story. It is a rather fascinating one, and I believe it to be true. In Japan, there is a fish called *fugu*, or pufferfish, whose organs contain a deadly toxin known as tetrodotoxin. Today, only licensed chefs may prepare it, and it is regarded as a delicacy of exquisite taste.

About five centuries ago, during the era of Toyotomi Hideyoshi, it is said that several samurai died from fugu poisoning. In response, the shogun issued a nationwide ban on eating fugu. The prohibition persisted through the Edo period, with strict punishments imposed by regional lords. In the Meiji era, an 1882 law even declared, "Those who eat fugu shall be detained or fined," making its consumption officially illegal.

Then, in 1888, when the ban was still in effect, Japan's first Prime Minister, Hirobumi Itō, visited a restaurant called *Shunpanrō* in Shimonoseki, Yamaguchi Prefecture. That evening, the restaurant had little fresh fish available except for live fugu swimming in its tanks. The chef, who had long practiced safe preparation in private, decided to take the risk and served the dish to the Prime Minister. Itō praised its taste, and from that event, the ban was lifted in Yamaguchi Prefecture. Aspiring chefs from all over Japan flocked to Shimonoseki to learn fugu cuisine, and soon the ban was lifted nationwide.[76]

What can we learn from this story? Even when facing something new and risky, thorough preparation builds confidence, and that confidence gives rise to bold action.

---

[76] Sekitora Honten. "The History of Shimonoseki's Fugu." *Fuku.ski,* 2025. https://www.fuku.ski/encyclopedia/history.

Seizing the right moment without hesitation. That, ultimately, is what leads to business success.

Today, the evolution of energy systems and AI are the great forces reshaping global markets, and the speed of change is astonishing. California's plan to achieve 100 percent electrification of passenger vehicles, for example, would require the equivalent output of five or six Diablo Canyon-sized nuclear plants. Meanwhile, data centers and AI infrastructure are expanding exponentially, consuming immense amounts of electricity.

Looking ahead, we must think carefully about how we wish to reshape the world. What products to develop, how to guide markets through short-term transitions, and how to build a sound global market in the process. The ability to identify the right products for both short-term and long-term horizons, and to develop them swiftly and effectively, is the essential skill of a global engineer.

The challenge is not an easy one. But by striving to understand market needs, building deep knowledge, and combining that with strong technical capability, you can rise to meet it. Whatever you are developing now, ask yourself: is it designed solely from an engineer's point of view? Are you imposing your creation on the market, or are you aligning with it? Reflect on how your development aligns with real needs. My hope is that you will become a global engineer who can confidently say that your work, your product, truly serves the world's needs.

And remember this: my unwavering insistence on introducing the right product to the market at the right time comes from a deeply held conviction that I hope you will truly take to heart.

Each careful decision you make, each product you continue to refine, and each sincere question you raise becomes a step toward shaping a better future. Even the smallest improvement you create today may become the spark that transforms an entire market tomorrow.

We must never underestimate the power of our curiosity, our persistence, and our compassion for people.

Engineers are not merely building devices or systems; they are creating possibilities themselves. You carry the unique responsibility of turning ideas into reality, influencing industries, and enriching the lives of people around the world.

For this reason, walk your path with pride, embrace the responsibility it carries, and move forward with confidence. There is a world that only you can bring into existence. And through your work, the world will surely become a better place.

Chapter 24

From AI Efficiency to Human Creativity: Entering the Artistic Realm of Engineering

Will may arise in AI;
emotions will not, for they are not required.
—Author

Have you ever heard the term *functional beauty*? It means that something with superior functionality is beautiful in appearance as well. Or, to put it another way, something that looks inelegant is unlikely to be functionally excellent either. Anyone who is an engineer has probably encountered this phrase before. Interpretations may vary, but essentially, a design that looks free of waste is also functionally efficient.

Of course, there are objects that fulfill their functions perfectly yet are not particularly beautiful. However, among products that meet the same functional requirements, those that are visually appealing sell better. Moreover, if the design is good, people will often choose that product even if its functionality is slightly inferior. That's how important appearance is. Something everyone can agree on. In other words, an engineer must also be an artist.

A beloved book, a beautiful piece of music, a magnificent painting, such experiences belong not to the realm of intellect but to emotion. When we encounter them, we feel pleasure, and from that pleasure springs the energy to live. At least, that's how I see it. The reason we always desire new things is because of this: products must appeal to human emotion.

To support the work of engineers who have these elements, can AI, which is now demonstrating its capabilities everywhere, move people emotionally? I believe the answer is almost certainly "no." The reason is that emotion lies beyond the domain of conscious control. AI may one day develop a kind of consciousness, but it will never reach the realm of emotion, because emotion is something necessary to humans but not to AI. To make people feel moved through a product remains the great challenge of AI. And I believe that only human engineers can achieve that.

Thus, I decided to ask an AI about the many questions I had encountered in the development and design of hydrogen fuel cells, and to examine the results.

My prompt to the AI (ChatGPT) was: "Teach me how to design a household-scale hydrogen power generator."

This was ChatGPT's response:

A. Overview of Required Considerations

- Hydrogen production (mainly electrolysis: electrolyzer)
- Hydrogen storage (compression, metal hydrides, chemical adsorption, etc. However, for household use, compressed tanks or external supply are common.)

- Power-generation unit (fuel cells such as PEMFC, or internal combustion engines when hydrogen is used as fuel)
- Power management (inverter, hybrid operation with batteries, control systems)
- Safety and monitoring systems (leak detection, ventilation, over-pressure protection, fire detection, emergency shutdown)
- Water supply and water treatment (purified water suitable for electrolysis)
- Exhaust and thermal management (utilization of fuel-cell waste heat and safe exhaust pathways)

B. Initial Decisions in the Design Process

- Purpose: backup power during outages, daily self-generation (off-grid), or experimental use of hydrogen fuel
- Power output requirements: necessary continuous output [kW] and required energy amount [kWh/day]
- Availability: required continuous operating hours; responsiveness (instant startup needed or not)
- Infrastructure conditions: installation site, ventilation (indoor/outdoor), surrounding environment, legal and municipal requirements
- Budget and maintenance framework: initial cost, operating cost, maintenance contracts

C. Conceptual Design Flow (Brief)

i. Energy balance estimation (rough calculation)
ii. Selection policy for major equipment (conceptual)
   - Electrolyzer, tank, generator, electrical system
iii. Safety design (mandatory)

  - Ventilation, leak detection, explosion-proof design, compliance with standards and codes

iv. Operation and maintenance

D. Representative Safety Standards and Code Compliance

- NFPA 2, ISO 19880-1, DOE / H2Tools / EPRI safety guidelines

E. Things to Avoid in the Design (Short List)

F. Practical Next Steps Toward Implementation

G. Methods for Preliminary Calculations

Even just the major categories produced a list of this size. In reality, each of these categories contains mid-level and detailed items. For example, under "methods for preliminary calculations," the energy-balance formulas to be used were listed, along with an explanation of what values could be computed from them.

Any engineer would immediately understand how greatly this kind of support can assist in establishing the technical foundation of a design.

Next, I asked a question in the emotional domain. That is, how to create the sense of appeal in a product.

My prompt to the AI (ChatGPT) was: "What kind of design would purchasers find appealing in a household-scale hydrogen power generator?"

This was ChatGPT's response:

A. A compact form that "fits naturally into the home"

- For household use, it is important that the product is not too large or too rugged, and that it blends into the everyday interior or exterior appearance of a home.

B. An interface with intuitive operability and clear visibility

- Panels or displays that allow users to instantly understand the power-generation status, remaining hydrogen, availability of hot water, and safety conditions (abnormalities, ventilation status, warnings, etc.).
- Switches, maintenance procedures, and fuel (or hydrogen) replenishment should be intuitive, allowing users with no technical knowledge to operate the system without confusion.

C. Attention to quietness and comfort

- Generators are generally associated with "noise, mechanical sounds, and vibration," but for household use, low noise and low vibration are highly attractive features.

D. Visualization of function and user experience—providing a sense of "self-sufficiency in energy"

E. Aesthetic and interior harmony—making it part of the home's design

- Whether installed behind an exterior wall, in a utility space, or inside a garage, users are more receptive when the unit is not a "bulky, conspicuous machine" but instead has an exterior that harmonizes with the house or remains discreet and smart.
- Through choices of color, surface finish (panels, covers), and form, the product can feel less like a machine and more like "a part of the home's infrastructure."

The answer to the former question regarding design methodology was quantitative in nature, something that will produce the same result regardless of who executes it. Consequently, this is a field that AI will eventually be able to handle almost entirely. In addition to data analysis, preparing documents and assisting with presentations and reports, I expect numerous aspects of the work I am currently involved in will eventually be supported by AI. There is no doubt that AI will even be capable of creating drawings and conducting prototyping through 3D printers.

In contrast, the answer to the latter question did indeed include good suggestions in terms of what points to pay attention to. However, all of the answers were qualitative, and quantitative answers vary entirely depending on market conditions, user preferences, and housing environments. This makes it clear that this is a field in which the abilities of human engineers are indispensable. In other words, rather than yielding a single scientifically correct answer, this field relies on the creative thinking and practical ingenuity of engineers to produce viable solutions.

Furthermore, the items (key points) presented by the AI in this example were all derived from past experience. It made no reference to elements that future purchasers might find appealing. The elements that past markets or users could not have imagined. And it did not even offer the suggestion that such considerations should be taken into account.

In this way, AI provides powerful support based on the accumulated achievements of engineers of the past, but it does not possess new ideas that have no precedent.

There is no doubt that the day when AI is fully utilized will come, and by leveraging AI, the volume and quality of technological development conducted by engineers will rise dramatically.

For that very reason, it goes without saying that engineers must retain the technical ability to discern incorrect answers produced by AI. The ability that, for now at least, still remains necessary. It is also our role as engineers to identify such AI mistakes and correct them, thereby enhancing its reliability.

Moreover, because AI provides fair and objective analyses and results, there is no doubt that it will serve as an extremely valuable mediator when conducting technical development within teams that include members from culturally different backgrounds, such as Japanese engineers.

It is undeniable that cultivating technological development capabilities in the artistic domain will require new, dedicated time. In that case, why not study prompt management to reduce the workload engineers currently expend, thereby creating time that has never before been available?

Now, with the time thus gained, I would like to turn to thinking about the development of products that appeal to the senses and emotions.

I have long been fond of Marc Chagall. The Marc Chagall. He was said to have been on good terms with Picasso, yet his expressions are completely different, painting the landscapes of the heart within a world of wonder.

When I first saw Chagall's paintings, the only word that came to mind was "mystery." Chickens, cows, violins, how was I supposed to interpret these? The colors were lovely, but nothing truly reached me.

Later, I happened to learn a little about Chagall, not so much about the artist himself, but about Jewish culture. I discovered that there are expressions like "so happy I could float in the air," "calm as playing a violin on a rooftop," and "as busy as needing seven fingers." Once I knew that, I could suddenly imagine: Chagall painting with seven fingers must have been incredibly busy; on his birthday, when Bella came to visit with flowers, he was so overjoyed he felt like floating in the air. The artist's heart began to reach me through his imagery.

What once seemed incomprehensible became deeply moving once I understood the cultural background behind it. My imagination joined his, and I found myself wondering, "Was he feeling this way? Or perhaps that way?" I began to see things from his point of view.

Many people call Chagall's blue "beautiful," but to me, it is not. That color often appears in works that convey anxiety, restlessness, or sadness. In *The Birthday*, where Bella suddenly appears holding flowers, there is no trace of blue. Nor is there any in *Over the Town*, a work from his later years, filled with colorful flowers and radiant with joy and eternal connection to Bella, who had once filled his life with applause and love.

I have had two remarkable experiences in my life that changed the way I understand art.

The first was at the arrival gate of Los Angeles Airport. Amid the bustling crowd, there was a landscape painting used as part of the interior decoration. As I gazed at it absentmindedly, I suddenly found myself drawn into the landscape and tears began to flow uncontrollably. It was the first time in my life that something like that had happened.

The second was in Ginza, Tokyo. I was enjoying my morning coffee at Starbucks when the *Pas de Deux* from *The Nutcracker* began to play over the speakers. Just the simple sequence of notes, *do-si-la-so-fa-mi-re-do,* was so beautiful that tears welled up again and wouldn't stop. The two people sitting across from me looked startled, as though they had witnessed something they shouldn't have, and quickly averted their eyes.

From these experiences, I came to understand that an artwork is not complete through the artist alone. It is completed when the viewer feels something. Whether it be awe, anger, or sorrow. It is an exchange of emotion across time and space. Works that many people call "great art" are those that stir emotion in many hearts.

What a piece of art conveys or perhaps, the emotions it evokes, differs from person to person, shaped by each individual's culture, knowledge, and background.

Let us become engineers who possess the ability to create products that allow many people, across different cultures and knowledge backgrounds, to perceive comfort and resonance through their senses as they experience our work.

Products that capture people's interest must not only embody functional beauty, that is, appeal to the senses, but also possess a touch of humor and uniqueness. AI, however, cannot joke. A joke made simply because a prompt said "be funny" will never be funny. Everyone knows that an explained joke is not amusing.

When Raphael painted *The School of Athens*, he secretly included himself, Michelangelo, and Leonardo da Vinci in the fresco. A playful gesture that still gives every viewer something to smile about. In Jacques-Louis David's *The Coronation of Napoleon*, the version displayed at Versailles shows a woman, believed to be Pauline, wearing a pink dress, while in the Louvre version, she wears the same uncolored attire as the other women. I've heard this was because a law at the time forbade creating identical versions of the same work. But why introduce such a "spot the difference" element? I believe it was the artist's little prank. His way of adding a unique twist for the viewer. Indeed, this very detail keeps the work the subject of endless discussion: "Napoleon adored Pauline most," some say, while others speculate, "David was secretly in love with her." Just as the artist intended.

It would be too valuable to confine such an attractive and witty concept solely to the world of artistic works. From here on, let us bring products into the world that are known for these very themes and that leave their mark on history.

Now, imagine a world overflowing with beautifully designed products. Everywhere you look, irresistible items that spark excitement the moment you see them. Images of products so captivating that they seem to flow directly from the device you wear. In such world, AI handles the functional, structural, and quality aspects, while engineers create the aesthetic and emotional appeal. The functional beauty that gives the product life.

A product that fulfills its purpose, meets quality standards, and is both well-designed and pleasant to use. Such a creation can only emerge from the collaboration between AI and human engineers. It is a partnership that draws out the best in both: AI's strengths in data and logic, and human engineers' strengths in emotion and creativity.

I look forward to the day when such collaborations fill the world with products that are not only functional but also endlessly delightful. Each one of them is a conversation piece that brings a smile.

Would you like me to explain why this joke is funny?
Y for yes, N for no.
Super AI

Chapter 25
Toward Tomorrow: Building the Future Together

There will be a future because we build it.
—Author

Throughout this book, I have explored how we, as Western engineers, can build effective teams with Japanese engineers working within the uniquely cross-cultural environment of Japan. Yet in truth, nothing has changed. Nor can anything change overnight. Many Japanese colleagues still refer to us as "they," and somewhere in your own mind you may find yourself whispering, "I don't trust them."

Even so, let us begin by accepting that this, too, is all right for now. As I have discussed in these pages, unless this situation improves, it will be difficult for you to fully demonstrate the abilities you truly possess. However, if you focus solely on the gap between the ideal and the present, your frustration will grow, stress will accumulate, and your work will suffer further. It becomes a downward spiral.

This book is simply advice drawn from my own experience; it does not claim to be the sole correct answer. Even without relying on it, you are already making the best and most sincere decisions you can every single day.

Our lives are a continuous sequence of choices. Looking back, you may occasionally think, *I should have done things differently then.* But let me ask you this: in any of those moments, did you ever choose your response carelessly? Whether in small matters or in important ones, if there has ever been even a single instance when you made a choice thoughtlessly, I would like to hear about it. And yet, when we truly reflect, most of us cannot recall such an experience. In reality, we are always making the best choices available to us at the time.

The situation you find yourself in today is the cumulative result of all those carefully considered choices. The very best form of where your efforts have brought you. This is true, and there is nothing whatsoever to regret. And this accumulation will continue.

The fact that you now hold a position in which you possess the significant ability and responsibility to shape tomorrow as an engineer is something you have earned through your own effort. And you will continue to be an engineer who carries that responsibility forward.

With that confidence in your heart, allow yourself to feel satisfaction with who you are today, and from there, turn your attention toward the things you would like to improve, one by one. If what you wish to improve is the quality of collaboration with the Japanese engineers you are working with now, then draw upon the experience you have already gained and take the actions you believe are best. If, in doing so, anything I have introduced in this book proves helpful, I encourage you to make use of it.

To continually elevate the quality of our work is, I believe, a fundamental obligation of every engineer who strives to envision and create a better future.

Around the world, there are many people who long to become engineers shaping the future but cannot, because they must secure their daily survival. If we, who *can* work in such fields today, remember that we do so on behalf of those who cannot, we can feel both the weight of our responsibility and the richness of our fortune. Can you see that what lies at the foundation is the mutual dependence and mutual trust shared among people around the world?

Our ancestors—*Homo sapiens*, who first appeared around 300,000 years ago—spent most of their time simply trying to secure food. After surviving the last Ice Age, they endured endless wars, diseases with no effective cures, and constant hunger, never certain they would live to see the next day. That, in essence, is a summary of human history.[77]

Even today, the total population of nations highly rated for economic power, living standards, education, healthcare, and political stability— generally referred to as developed countries, for example, OECD (Organization for Economic Cooperation and Development) member countries —amounts to roughly 1.4 billion people, only about 17 percent of the global population.

For those of us, including you reading this book, who do not have to worry about food or survival tomorrow, it is no exaggeration to call that a *miracle-level happiness*.

We must recognize our responsibility to pass that happiness to future generations and to extend it as widely as possible across the world. We are fortunate to work on such

---

[77] Smithsonian National Museum of Natural History. "Our Species Arose at Least 300,000 Years Ago." *The Smithsonian Institution's Human Origins Program*, June 8, 2017. https://humanorigins.si.edu/research/whats-hot-human-origins/our-species-arose-least-300000-years-ago.

technologies that can reduce carbon dioxide emissions and lower global energy consumption.

To be engaged, as an individual human being, in engineering that builds the future is in itself a privilege and realizing that brings a deep awareness of happiness.

Look up at the blue sky. Touch the green of the mountains. Feel the gentleness of the sea. Think of the many species now facing extinction. As James Lovelock of the UK proposed, perhaps Earth itself is striving to preserve this nature.[78]

To aid in the effort to protect life on this planet and make human society more livable for future generations, who else but us engineers can take on that role? If we, the engineers, do not rise to the challenge, then who will?

To fulfill that responsibility, partnering with Japanese engineers is the best possible choice, and there is no doubt that such a collaboration would become the strongest team capable of shaping the world of tomorrow. Although these words come from the inevitably limited perspective of my own experience, they are the conclusion I have reached through the many years I have devoted to this work, and I can say with confidence that they reflect my genuine conviction.

[78] Lovelock, James. "Papers by James Lovelock." *Jameslovelock.org*, 2025. https://www.jameslovelock.org/papers/.

Epilogue

Having chosen engineering as my profession, I have spent much of my life traveling between Japan and the United States, and within the US itself. I wrote many of these reflections aboard airplanes or shinkansen trains during those journeys, and have finally managed to bring them together in this form.

People from different backgrounds, cultures, and languages form teams with a shared goal: to develop products that bring joy to the world. Along the way, we misunderstand one another, we argue, and yet, when a new product is completed, we share in the same joy of success before setting out again to create the next.

I have spent many years in such workplaces, working alongside people from diverse nations and environments. I have seen how differences in habits and ways of thinking can create misunderstandings, which sometimes damage relationships that could have otherwise flourished.

Through this, I learned that people can hurt others but also heal them. Surrounded by wonderful colleagues, I have been able to continue enriching my life. I am deeply grateful, and I wrote this book believing it is now my turn to share that happiness and to help engineers struggling with cultural differences.

In this book, I have mainly encouraged American engineers to set aside their own cultural assumptions and strive to understand the Japanese way of thinking to adjust themselves accordingly. Of course, Japanese engineers should also learn about American culture and values and show mutual respect. I am not saying that Americans must always adapt to the Japanese side.

However, most Japanese grow up entirely within Japanese culture, speaking only Japanese in their daily lives. Although there is talk of "global awareness," opportunities for true cross-cultural engagement remain limited and many understandably struggle with English.

Therefore, to work effectively with such team members, Americans must both adapt to Japanese ways and find ways to clearly convey Western concepts in ways their Japanese colleagues can grasp. That requires two-way communication. Not one-way. Both sides must be prepared: the speaker to express things accurately, and the listener to understand with care. To achieve that, a relationship of quality is essential.

I know people who, even when referred to as "they," are trusted individually. People say, "If *he* or *she* says it, I believe it." That is what I call a relationship of quality.

After working at a Japanese-affiliated company in the US for ten or twenty years, I have often been told by Japanese "You've become American," and by Americans, "Well, you're Japanese, after all." Using that in-between position, I have continued to explain Western ways to Japanese and Japanese ways to Americans. I don't know if it has always been effective, but I have always tried to build relationships of genuine trust.

In such a position where people might easily ask "Whose side are you on?", maintaining good relationships requires effort beyond the ordinary. I have always tried to keep promises, and when I couldn't, I explained why. I have shown my weaknesses as they are, and asked for help when I needed it. I have been open about what I wanted to do, what I could do, and what I could not.

These are just a few of the things I have tried to practice, and I would like to think they have helped build trust whether with Japanese or Americans.

Japanese people often struggle to speak frankly, tending to soften their words out of consideration for others. Americans, by contrast, tend to be cautious before trusting people. Perhaps that's a biased view based on my experience, but I believe such tendencies often lie at the root of misunderstandings.

I wish Japanese people would practice speaking a little more directly and clearly, without wrapping their words. What may be understood between Japanese people will not necessarily be understood by Americans. Conversely, I hope Americans can lower their guard a little and trust the Japanese more. Japanese people are not as calculating as Americans sometimes imagine.

Everything ultimately comes down to mutual trust. When we share the same goal, make the effort to understand one another, and take the time to explain ourselves, we deepen our mutual understanding. When problems arise or when things do not go the way we hoped, it is not because one side is at fault. Instead, it is an opportunity for both sides to work together and gain experience in resolving challenges as a team.

A relationship built on mutual trust cannot be created overnight. It may require patience, but without question, it is worth the time and effort it takes to build.

If you have learned something from what I've written, and if you feel inclined to try it to see whether it helps you achieve better results when working with Japanese engineers, then by all means, please try.

As for me, I hope to continue spending the years ahead surrounded by the wonderful people in my life, especially my wife, who is always closest to me, and to live happily and comfortably, day by day.

About the Author

Takehito Yokoo is an engineer, clean energy innovator, and cross-cultural leader with more than forty years of experience advancing sustainable technology and global collaboration.

As CEO of Jozen Power LLC, he leads initiatives in renewable energy and decarbonization. In addition, as president of the Global Engineers Initiative, he cultivates engineers with a global perspective, blending Japanese precision and American innovation to help build a businesscommunity that contributes meaningfully to the world.

Before founding Jozen Power and the Global Engineers Initiative, Yokoo spent more than three decades at Toyota Motor North America R&D. where he served as powertrain chief engineer and senior executive engineer of advanced fuel cell. He led Toyota's hybrid, battery-electric, and hydrogen fuel cell programs and launched the world's first OEM hydrogen fuel cell heavy-duty truck demonstration at the Port of Los Angeles in 2017.

In 2021, he co-founded the Japan Hydrogen Forum (JH2F) in collaboration with the Japan External Trade Organization and the Consulate-General of Japan in Los Angeles, promoting cooperation between Japan and the United States on hydrogen business and decarbonization. He continues to serve as an advisor to the forum.

In 2025, Yokoo was awarded the Consul General's Commendation by the Consulate-General of Japan in Los Angeles in recognition of his efforts to promote the Japan–US hydrogen business.

Yokoo is also a Senior Managing Director at ENSO Infrastructure, where he drives the practical use of hydrogen technologies in the United States, and a member of the Advisory Council of Stanford University's Precourt Institute for Energy, part of the Stanford Doerr School of Sustainability.

He holds a Master of Science in mechanical engineering from Hosei University in Tokyo. Now in the next chapter of his career, Yokoo is dedicated to sharing the lessons of cross-cultural collaboration he learned as a global engineer. Through his leadership and training initiatives, he helps professionals and organizations build bridges between innovation, culture, and purpose.

Outside of work, Yokoo enjoys mountain biking on nearby trails and playing the piano. He currently resides in Los Angeles, USA.